BECOMING A MORE EFFECTIVE TEACHER

Master Teaching Edition

Live to Teach - Teach Them to Live

MASTER TEACHING EDITION

WHITE MARLIN MEDIA
Live to read – Read to Live.

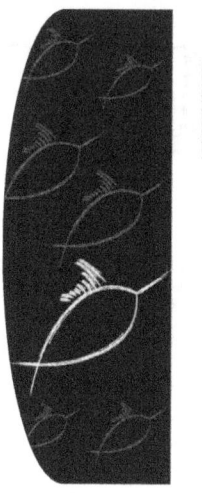

Michael L. Donaldson M.S. All rights reserved. No part of this publication may be reproduced or transmitted in any form or by any means electronic or mechanical, including photocopy, recording, or any information storage and retrieval system, without permission in writing from both the copyright owner and the publisher.

    Requests for permission to make copies of any part of this work should be mailed to Permissions Department, White marlin Media, P.O. Box 356, Joelton Tn. 37080.

Copyright 2018, 2005 - White Marlin Media

ISBN: 978-09764645-8-7

Unless otherwise stated, all scriptures come from the King James Version.

TABLE OF CONTENTS

About the author……………………………………………………………..9
About this book……………………………………………………………..11
From the author's desk ……………………………………………………..12

Section 1.0 - Biblical leadership…………………………………………14
       1.1 God's Plan……………………………………………………15
       1.2 The Calling on its face………………………………………..16
       1.3 The reason for it all…………………………………………..16
       1.4 Edifying the body (the mystery) ……………………………..16
       1.5 Human Resources Management Model……………………….17
       1.6 Rank in the Kingdom…………………………………………17
       1.7 Division of labor……………………………………………..18
       1.8 The Tabernacle/Temple Construct…………………………...18
       1.9 The Church Construct………………………………………..18
    1.11 Types of authority………………………………………………19
    1.11 Where leaders get their authority……………………………….23
    1.12 The warning to teacher………………………………………….31
    1.13 Warnings about teachers………………………………………..33
    1.14 The purpose of credentials……………………………………...37
    1.15 Caiaphastics……………………………………………………..41

Section 2.0 - Becoming a more effective Teacher……………………….42
    2.0 A definition of Teacher…………………………………………...43
    2.1 What a lesson should entail……………………………………….43
    2.2 What makes an effective teacher?………………………………..43
    2.3 Necessary tools for a teacher……………………………………..46

Section 3.0 - Becoming a more effective Pastor ………………………...48
    3.0 A definition of Pastor……………………………………………..49
    3.1 Typical pastoral duties…………………………………………….49
    3.2 What a pastoral lesson should entail……………………………...51
    3.3 What makes an effective pastor…………………………………..53
    3.4 The necessary tools for a pastor…………………………………..56
    3.5 Questions for pastoral candidates…………………………………58

TABLE OF CONTENTS

Section 4.0 - Becoming a more effective Prophet..................................62
    4.0 A definition of Prophet...63
        4.1.1 Typical prophetic duties..63
        4.1.2 Prophetic personality traits....................................64
    4.2 A warning about prophets and familiar spirits........................65
        4.2.1 #51 Warnings about familiar spirits.......................65
    4.3 What a prophetic lesson should entail...................................75
    4.4 What makes an effective prophet? 79
    4.5 Modular questions for prophet candidates............................81

Section 5.0 - Becoming a more effective Evangelist............................86
    5.0 A definition of Evangelist 87
    5.1 Typical evangelical duties...87
    5.2 What an evangelistic lesson should entail.............................89
    5.3 What makes an effective evangelist....................................91
    5.4 Tools necessary for evangelists..93
    5.5 Evangelical candidate questions...95

Section 6.0 - Becoming a more effective Deacon................................98
    6.0 A definition of Deacon..99
    6.2 Typical deacon responsibilities and duties............................99
    6.3 What deacon should teach..100
    6.4 What makes an effective deacon.......................................101
    6.5 Necessary deacon tools..103
    6.6 Questions for the deacon candidates..................................105

Section 7.0 - Becoming a more effective Elder / Bishop / Overseer............108
    7.0 A definition of Elder..109
    7.2 Typical elder responsibilities and duties..............................109
    7.3 What elders should teach..111
    7.4 What makes an effective elder...113
    7.5 Necessary elder tools..115
    7.6 Questions for elder candidates...116

TABLE OF CONTENTS

Section 8.0 - Becoming a more effective Apostle....................118
    8.1 A definition of apostle..119
    8.2 Basic qualifications of an apostle.............................119
    8.3 Development of the apostolic calling........................121
    8.4 What Apostolic lessons should contain.....................124
    8.5 What Apostolic lessons should not contain................126
    8.6 What makes a more effective apostle........................127
    8.7 Necessary tools for an apostle.................................131
    8.8 Warnings about false apostles..................................133
    8.9 Modular questions for apostle candidates..................136

Section 9.0 - Learning the styles of the audience....................138
    9.0 Learning the styles of the audience...........................141
    9.2 Learning Styles..142
        9.2.1 The Dynamic learning style.........................142
        9.2.2 The Dialectical learning style......................143
        9.2.3 The Didactic learning style.........................144
        9.2.4 The Demonstrative learning style.................145
        9.2.5 The Animated learning style.......................146
        9.2.6 The Empirical learning style.......................147
        9.2.7 The Abstract learning style........................148
        9.2.8 The Argumentative learning style................149
        9.2.9 The Linguistic learner................................150
        9.2.10 The Naturalist.......................................151
        9.2.11 The Auditory...152
        9.2.12 The Kinesthetic learner............................153
        9.2.13 The Visual or Spatial learner....................154
        9.2.14 The Logical or Mathematical learner.........155
        9.2.15 The Interpersonal learner.........................156
        9.2.16 The Intrapersonal learner.........................157
        9.2.17 Apologetic learning style.........................158
        9.2.18 The Exploration learning style..................159
        9.2.19 The Confrontational learning style............160
        9.2.20 The Testimonial learning style.................161

TABLE OF CONTENTS

    9.2.21 The Reciprocal learning style...................................162
    9.2.22 The Task learning style..163
    9.2.23 The Problem-Solving learning style.........................164
    9.2.24 The Invitational learning style................................165
    9.2.25 The Service learning style......................................166
    9.2.26 The Command learning style.................................167
    9.2.27 Practical learning style...168
    9.2.28 Guided Discovery learning style.............................169
    9.2.29 The Atheist...170
        9.29.1 Methods suggested in dealing with Atheists,
                Fundamentalists, and Cynics..........................171
        9.29.2 Reasons suggested for Failure in dealing with
                Atheists, Fundamentalists, and Cynics............171

Section 10.0 - The Teacher's Assessment Center.....................174
    10.1 Teaching Styles...175
        10.1.2 The Dynamic Style..177
        10.1.3 The Dialectical Style..178
        10.1.4 The Didactic style..179
        10.1.5 The Demonstrative Style...180
        10.1.6 The Animated Style...181
        10.1.7 The Empirical Style...182
        10.1.8 The Abstract Style...183
        10.1.9 The Argumentative Style...184
        10.1.10 The Command Style..185
        10.1.11 The Practical Style...186
        10.1.12 The Reciprocal Style..187
        10.1.13 The Task Style...188
        10.1.14 The Guided Discovery Style..................................189
        10.1.15 The Problem-Solving Style....................................190
        10.1.16 The Exploration Style...191
        10.1.17 The Confrontational Style......................................192
        10.1.18 The Testimonial Style...193
        10.1.19 The Interpersonal Style..194

TABLE OF CONTENTS

    10.1.20 The Invitational Style……………………………………..195
    10.1.21 The Service Style……………………………………………196
    10.1.22 The Apologetic Style…………………………………………197
10.2 Strengths and weaknesses of the Teaching Styles……………. …198
    10.2.1 The Dynamic Style…………………………………………...200
    10.2.2 The Dialectical Style………………………………………….201
    10.2.3 The Didactic Style…………………………………………….202
    10.2.4 The Demonstrative Style……………………………………...203
    10.2.5 The Animated Style…………………………………………...204
    10.2.6 The Empirical Style…………………………………………...205
    10.2.7 The Abstract Style…………………………………………….206
    10.2.8 The Argumentative Style……………………………………...207
    10.2.9 The Apologetic Style………………………………………….208
    10.2.10 The Exploration Style……………………………………….209
    10.2.11 The Confrontational Style…………………………………...210
    10.2.12 The Testimonial Style……………………………………….211
    10.2.13 The Reciprocal Style………………………………………...212
    10.2.14 The Task Style……………………………………………....213
    10.2.15 The Problem-Solving Style………………………………….214
    10.2.16 The Invitational Style……………………………………….215
    10.2.17 The Interpersonal Style……………………………………...216
    10.2.18 The Service Style……………………………………………217
    10.2.19 The Command Style…………………………………………218
    10.2.20 Practical Style……………………………………………….219
    10.2.21 Guided Discovery Style……………………………………..220
10.3 Style determination…………………………………………………221
    10.3.1 A way to determine your style………………………………..222
    10.3.2 Dynamic style determination………………………………….224
    10.3.3 Dialectical style determination ……………………………….225
    10.3.4 Didactic style determination…………………………………..226
    10.3.5 Demonstrative style determination …………………………...227
    10.3.6 Animated style determination ………………………………...228
    10.3.7 Empirical style determination ………………………………...229
    10.3.8 Abstract style determination ………………………………….230

TABLE OF CONTENTS

    10.3.9 Argumentative style determination 231
    10.3.10 Apologetic style determination 232
    10.3.11 Exploration style determination 233
    10.3.12 Confrontational style determination 234
    10.3.13 Testimonial style determination 235
    10.3.14 Reciprocal style determination 236
    10.3.15 Task style determination 237
    10.3.16 Problem-solving style determination 238
    10.3.17 Invitational style determination 239
    10.3.18 Interpersonal style determination 240
    10.3.19 Intrapersonal style determination.........................241
    10.3.20 Service style determination 242
    10.3.21 Command style determination 243
    10.3.22 Practical style determination 244
    10.3.23 Guided Discovery style determination 245
  10.4 Common teaching mistakes……………………………...246

Section 11.0 - More effective lessons………………………….256
  11.1 How to develop a plan………………………………….257
  11.2 Writing a plan…………………………………………..260
  11.3 Effective lesson plan components……………………...265
  11.4 Importance of color and shapes in effective lesson plans………..267

Section 12.0 - The Spiritual skills……………………..............269
  12.1 The Spiritual skills……………………………………...270
  12.2 Understanding the Spiritual skills..…………………….272
  12.3 The spiritual skills assessment………………………….275

Bibliography - Becoming a more effective teacher…………………….283

About the Author

Evangelist Michael Donaldson was born in Nassau Bahamas, where he attended a Methodist school and a Pentecostal church and accepted Christ when he was 14yrs old. Due to his mother's Missional activities, Donaldson spent hundreds of hours of his youth feeding and clothing the less fortunate, learning and teaching the word.

Donaldson moved to the United States of America in 1987 where for the next seven years he contributed precious little to the Kingdom of Heaven. Since returning to Kingdom service in 1995 teaching Spiritual Warfare and making both Disciple-makers and Disciples.

Donaldson is CEO of Ashara Ministries[1] Charter Family. The motto of Ashara is, *"Building people not churches."* Under that mission, Ashara has developed numerous programs to teach and reach lost sheep.

Donaldson has Certificate of Theology from Falwell University, a Master of Science in Public Administration - Policy, and Planning from Cumberland University, where he was inducted into Pi Gamma Mu Int'l Honor Society in Social Science and a B.S. in Political Science, (Pres. Dorm Council, Student Union Board of Governors, Food Services Committee, Student Court, and spending numerous semesters on the Nat'l Dean's List). His list of published works consists of;

- From a Fishing Trip in Patmos
- From a Fishing Trip in Patmos: Disciple-Maker's Edition
- The Lights in Patmos
- From a Fortress in Patmos
- Honeymoon in Patmos
- Black Coffee
- The Butterfly Veil
- From a War in Patmos
- Becoming a More Effective Teacher: Teaching Master's Edition

I believe, "There is beauty in all of God's children which manifests itself in their expression of His love. The only true church of Christ exists in the hearts of His people. The edifices we build fail in comparison to give glory and honor to the Lord God almighty. The love of God shows itself in the hearts of His people; Only this dwelling place lasts forever. This is not because man last forever, but because God lasts forever. Remember, only what we do for Christ will last."

I use a philosophy when I teach; it is something learned whilst attaining my 3rd Degree Black Belt in Wado-Ryu Karate. It is to this philosophy I dedicate this work and the teachings of my life.

"A Masterpiece; A piece created by a master, is only a masterpiece when the viewer sees what the Master wants the student to see."

When we teach, we must be effective and compliant. WE MUST PAINT THE PICTURE THE FATHER WANTS HIS PEOPLE TO SEE, anything else is accursed.

About this Resource

"**And He said unto them, 'Unto you it is given to know the mystery of the kingdom of God: but unto them that are without, all *these* things are done in parables**." (Mark 4:34).

By necessity, this resource has many components. Extensive citations because it is a summation of years of study across all sides of ecumenical teaching to point out the best information available. This is part work-book, part reference guide, mostly teaching aid. This resource is a teaching aid, which is a tool for classrooms, seminars. This resource functions best for onboarding and internal promotion, assignment, and maturation. In order that we become more effective teachers we need to do a better job of understand that teaching has components; three to be exact.

Verily I say that they do not exist separately, they only exist to interact with each other. God did not ordain a lesson with no students, nor a student without a teacher.

For the perfecting of the saints He ordained a Triune Learning System© which is all about Him. "**Son though he was, he learned obedience from what he suffered**."

- The Lesson - How could He learn but there was a lesson?
- The Teacher - How could there be a lesson but there was no Teacher.
- The Student - And why then obedience lest He was also a Student.

Together we look at teaching styles, teaching goals, lesson development, understanding and developing students and learning how to teach ourselves.

This resource brings to life the secret to becoming a more effective teacher, by bringing the lessons, the student, and the teacher all back into the will and the way of God.

From the Author's Desk

The afore mentioned qualifications give information about me; they do not to serve as validation. They give an example of some basic signs of effort that we should look for in all God's servants. Credentials do not indicate spirituality, they speak to stewardship and dedication. Credentials only matter when His Spirit is not present; in His presence we all dim and must kneel.

In case the question arises, as to how I am qualified to produce this resource; the answer is easy. When someone earns a Master's Degree, they are recognized as having enough knowledge in a field of study to be called a Master of or in the field. That's why the correct way to write Master's Degree is with an apostrophe - "it is the Conferred degree of a Master[3]". I do not have a Master's in Divinity, but there exists no requisite for this in the Scriptures. What I do have a Master's Degree in is Stewardship.

Here is what my Mastery entails;

- Accounting
- Intercultural Business Practices
- Business Law
- Corporate Communications
- Corporate Finance
- Economics
- Energy
- Entrepreneurship
- Ethical Decision Making
- Financial Reporting
- Human Resource Management
- Information Technology
- International Business
- Investments
- Leadership
- Motivation
- Marketing
- Marketing Research
- Operational Research
- Operations and Logistics
- Public Relations
- Statistics
- Strategic Management
- Supply Chain Management
- Workplace Security

I was not called to Master Divinity, God commissioned us to **teach what He commanded**[4]. Therefore, a degree in managing and administering the tasks of my calling qualify me to write about the things He commanded us to fulfil.

The Bible admonishes us to teach; I shall, I do. If you want to challenge this resource, start with, "In the beginning…" and end at "…The grace of our Lord Jesus Christ be with you all. Amen." Between these words lay my credentials, and my accreditation.

Michael L Donaldson M.S.

1.0

BIBLICAL LEADERSHIP

"Be sure you know the condition of your flocks, give careful attention to your herds; for riches do not endure forever, and a crown is not secure for all generations." (Proverbs 27:23-24 NIV).

1.0
BIBLICAL LEADERSHIP

"**And God hath set some in the church, first apostles, secondarily prophets, thirdly teachers, after that miracles, then gifts of healings, helps, governments, diversities of tongues**." (1 Corinthians 3:28).

The phrase 'good and faithful servant' has a clear undertone to it. Clearly veiled in the phrase lies the model for Biblical leadership. God called us into liberty; not to use liberty for an occasion to please the flesh, but to love and serve one another. The leader is not called to lord over (that is God's job), but to serve God as a Shepherd (manager) of God's flock. You can have sheep with no shepherd, but not the other way around.

There is ABSOLUTELY NO REASON for there to be confusion about in whose house we serve and consequently Whom it is we serve. Luke 2:49 and John 14:2,3 are clear and concise that we serve in someone else's House. The house we serve in has a ruler and has rules. God did not call us to set rules, but clearly to manage by His rules and instruct in His way of living.

We look at other scriptures John 3:49, John 8:28, and we see that even Jesus SAID ONLY WHAT HIS FATHER SAID, He added nothing to the text. How dare we claim to serve in truth, when we do not truly serve the King, in the manner He requires. If we do not heed His rules, we commit treason against the King.

John 14:15 and Luke 13:27, and Matthew 3:30 bear out that God fully expects those who serve Him and under Him to do so at His behest and bidding. There is no new move of God, no new gospel, nothing new under the Son; For what He set, He set to be perfect (1 Corinthians 13:9).

1.1 GOD'S PLAN

Ephesians 4 lays out His plan for His kingdom. In God's assembly plan, He is building and maintaining Kingdom; NOT THE CHURCH. The church is a part of God's Kingdom, it is a normative, innocuous, entry point for everyone from the darkness into His Light.

Just as an emergency room knows no boundaries nor any hours, the buildings we erect, are not storehouses for souls, they are not to house souls, they are for perfecting His people, so they can go out and do HIS and only His will.

1.2 THE CALLING ON ITS FACE[5]

The components of our calling are to walk (serve) with;
1. Lowliness (Humility)
2. Meekness (Self-control)
3. Longsuffering (Patience)
4. Forbearing one another in love (Forgiveness)
5. God then admonishes us to endeavor to keep the unity of the Spirit in the bond of peace (Peace and unity).

As we are prone to forget, the Bible reminds us, that there is;
1. One body
2. One Spirit
3. One hope of the calling
4. One Lord
5. One faith
6. One baptism
7. One God and Father of all, who is above all

1.3 THE REASON FOR IT ALL

To and for His plan God ordained resources. But He says what the resources do and why. It is only for His reasons the resources exist and thrive. These tasks and skill areas He gave for the express purposes of;
1. The perfecting of the saints
2. The work of the ministry
3. The edifying of the body of Christ

Although, listed separately, these are not three purposes, they are one. The mission of the Kingdom manager is to build and maintain His Kingdom. Therefore, these three are not exclusive, but mutually dependent, as they complement and complete His singular will FOREVER[6].

1.4 EDIFYING THE BODY (The Mystery)

Edifying the body is clear and concisely laid out as the Managers job to stop His Sheep from carried about with every wind of doctrine, by the sleight of men, and cunning craftiness, whereby they lie in wait to deceive.

In other words, our jobs are more perfunctory than Scholastic. He charged us to repeat His commands, not to transliterate them. It is not literacy Jesus learned from His study of the scripture or efface, but obedience (Hebrews 5:8). This is a Kingdom Mystery.

God perfected and completed the work, we are not doing that function we are simply trying to get as many people to;
1. Accept Him as King (Psalms 23).
2. Then they learn to work out their own salvation (righteousness). with fear and trembling (Philippians 2:3).
3. Move through the perfecting states (Romans 5:3-4).
4. And on into love (Matthew 5:48) (John 14:11).

God thought of His Kingdom and set about a plan to last until He returns. He set in place a plan to ensure management of His Kingdom until His return. Despite rhetoric He is not a cruel task master collecting from places He has not sewn. For He both descended and ascended to establish His order in the earth.

1.5 **HUMAN RESOURCES MANAGEMENT MODEL**

For His kingdom God established a Seven-Tiered Human Resources Management Model©;
1. Apostles
2. Prophets
3. Evangelists
4. Pastors (Shepherds)
5. Teachers
6. Elders
7. Deacon

_____
_____
_____
_____
_____
_____

1.6 **RANK IN THE KINGDOM**

While there is no actually rank in kingdom work, prophecy requires different facet of responsibility. Sadly; however, these two staples of the church always fall tasked as menial. There are only two set immovable offices in the church Elder and Deacon. These positions are fixed because they are perfunctory areas of responsibility, inside the operation for the factory.

1.7 DIVISION OF LABOR

The lack of rank does not mean that there is not a division of labor. Even in Heaven, each of the nine choirs (types of angel) controls a facet of kingdom work. Referred to as Choirs not just because they sing to the Lord, but because they sing to the Lord in unison. Each segment part of the Choir carrying only 1/9th of the tune, tempo, and melody. This harmony is what God looks for in His people[7].

1.8 DIVISION OF LABOR AND THE TABERNACLE/TEMPLE CONSTRUCT[8]

1. The Outer Court - A courtyard open to everybody {Elders}
2. The Inner Court - An inner courtyard restricted to priests and those with sacrifices {Elders, Teachers}
3. The Holy of Holies - Restricted only to priests

1.9 DIVISION OF LABOR AND THE CHURCH CONSTRUCT

Under the Church Construct, set up by Jesus after His ascension there are still three components to the Church, but the breakdown is different. The division is primarily inside the church and outside the church. The Holy of Holies relationship is access to all due to the Holy Spirit.

We often find three functionaries outside the walls of the church they operate freely. The reason they free float is because God's true church has no walls. As we move through this resource, upon completion you should be able to identify the division of labor and the functions of each tier.

Outside the walls of the Temple
- Apostles
- Prophets
- Evangelists

Inside the Temple
- Pastors (Shepherds)
- Teachers
- Elders
- Deacon
- Apostles
- Prophets
- Evangelists

1.11
TYPES OF AUTHORITY[9]

"Jesus answered, Thou couldest have no power at all against me, except it were given thee from above…" (John 19:11).

The word 'authority' occurs 37 times in 34 verses in the KJV of the Bible. Through the Bible the term has many applications. Let us loot at the various usages of the term in the Bible using Strong's Numbers[10]; then look at the types of Authority common to in leadership models.

This study it to help us understand that men have no real authority in the church. God is the Head of the church and her sole judge[11]. Is He alone not responsible for presenting her without spot or blemish? Like the best man in Biblical days, our task is to watch the door and windows on the honeymoon to protect the couple and their privacy. Make no mistake, we are not invited into the bed chamber, nor given to lay with the bride; that is for the Husband, for she is His bride.

1. H8633[12] - Authority, power, strength, energy
2. H7235 - Be or become great, be or become many, be or become much, be or become numerous
3. G1849 - Power of choice, liberty of doing as one pleases
4. G2715 - To exercise authority, wield power
5. G2468 - Give thyself wholly to
6. G1850 - To have power or authority, use power to be master of any
   - One, exercise authority over one to be master of the body to have full and entire authority over the body to hold the body subject to one's will to be brought under the power of anyone
7. G5247 - Elevation, pre-eminence, superiority
8. G831 - One who with his own hands kills another or himself one one who acts on his own authority, autocratic an absolute master to govern, exercise dominion over one
9. G2003 - An injunction, mandate, command the power or right to give orders, make decisions, and enforce obedience

From Secular Models we find other types of Authority. These types of authority occur in the church as well, but the church considers them worldly in nature.
1. **Rational-Legal Authority** - Elected officials
2. **Traditional Authority** - Customs, habits, and social structures
3. **Charismatic Authority** - Popular and powerful people, who others tend to follow and admire
4. **Illegitimate Authority** - Not legal, most often abusive and deceitful
5. **Perceived Authority** - Power though to exist that is not real or enforceable

As mentioned, here are apparently #9 types (choirs) of Angels[13]. God uses specific types of angels to do specific things. Rank does not indicate a good angel or bad angel, just as the term *teacher* is universal, and means nothing angel just implies heavenly host[14].

Although the Cherub does not appear to be the highest rank, God uses them to guard His throne and the way to the Tree of Life because they proved to be the most reliable. The evidence for this exists in Judges 9, Ezekiel 28, and Ezekiel 31.

God uses angels for war, wrath, retrieve bodies, guide and rescue people, transport people, to go with Him {Old Testament} to places here on earth. Cherubs are Kingdom angels, they do not serve a particular King.
1. **Seraphim**[15] (Seraphs) - Are the highest order of angels - (Isaiah 6:2-6, Revelations 4:8)
2. **Cherubim** (Cherubs) - Cherubim rank after the Seraphim - (Ezekiel 1)
3. **Thrones** - are the angels of humility, peace, and submission - (Colossians 1:16, Revelations 4:2)
4. **Dominions** - Are angels of leadership; - (Ephesians 1:21, Colossians 1:16)
5. **Virtues** - Translated from Greek word Might. Known as the Spirits of Motion and control the elements. Ephesians 1:21)
6. **Powers** - Warrior Angels - (Ephesians 1:21)
7. **Archangels** - Are generally taken to mean 'chief or leading angel' - (Jude 1:9)

8. **Principalities** - Spiritual beings hostile to God and human beings - (Romans 8:38, Ephesians 1:21).
9. **Angels** - Angels are closest to the natural world and Human beings. They deliver the prayers to God and God's answers and other messages to humans - (Romans 8:38)

When an earthly king dies the new king does not fire everybody in the army, the palace guard, cooks, police etc. They replace those closest to the king with friends and supporters, but the kingdom continues to function because of certain office held by faithful people. It is of this office 'duty' the Bible speaks fondly and succinctly. Those who maintain God's Temple work for the Temple King, not the manager of the earthly house.

Deacons and Elders are such, they serve God by safeguarding His kingdom. Deacons and Elders have no charge to develop or spread the kingdom - they safeguard God's sheep. So, there will and should be times that the deacon and the pastors or evangelists differ. Did not the angels differ, some wanted to follow God others wanted to follow Satan[16]? Deacons must stand for the flock and not the pastor. Elders and Deacons must keep their love for people in their care above, their friendship or respect for the pastor.

Pastors and teachers are part of the Internal kingdom staff, but they are to focus more on the perfecting tasks than safeguarding. Prophets and Apostles are Kingdom staff they are not permanent Temple staff as there are more like regional directors supporting integrity in the teachings of the various temples. Evangelists are external staff they have no temple duties.

___
___
___
___
___
___
___
___
___

1.12
WHERE LEADERS GET THEIR AUTHORITY

"**And Jesus came and said to them, 'All authority in heaven and on earth has been given to me. Go therefore and make disciples of all nations, baptizing them in the name of the Father and of the Son and of the Holy Spirit, and teaching them to obey everything that I have commanded you**'" (Matthew 28:18-28).

All leaders in the Bible get their anointing from the same source. If this is not true, if you think your calling is higher than another's, or that it came from a different spirit, then you are serving the wrong God.

1 Corinthians 3:5-7 lays down two more important facets of the Kingdom service. We see the that there are different ministrations but only one God and the ministrations are to profit all. The call and anointing are not only without repentance, they exist to help everyone.

Therefore, we all work for the same God, to the same end. Unless you are a doer of iniquity, in which case we rejoice that we walk a different path than you. The word used in Greek to imply ministrations is where we get two familiar words, *Administrate* and *Minister*. Time invariably separated the two meanings because men tried to separate from God; but they are inseparable:

- Service, ministering
- Of those who by the command of God proclaim and promote religion among men
- Of the office of Moses
- Of the office of the apostles and its administration
- Of the office of prophets, evangelists, elders etc.
- The ministration of those who render to others the offices of Christian affection especially those who help

meet need by either collecting or distributing of charities
- The office of the deacon in the church
- The service of those who prepare and present food[17]

Hopefully we have dispensed with the needs to waste further words establishing what you agreed to and signed off on when you accepted the call. Now we can study the traits of some of the most successful managers[18].

1.12.1 Successful managers create structure - Remember we are managing a Kingdom already established with rules and protocols, we are not creating a new kingdom - (John 14:7).

1.12.2 Successful managers use intuition - Trying the spirit by the Spirit and let His conscience be our guide. We never have to guess, or wonder about our calling, even when we walk away from it - (1 Peter 5:8).

1.12.3 Successful managers rely on knowledge - Our knowledge base only covers what the King reveals. There is no knowledge of value without Him and never kingdom knowledge not from Him (Exodus 31:3).

1.12.4 Successful managers believe in commitment - Be

committed to two things Live the right thing teach the right thing. Living the right thing, will develop the teacher in you, but the reciprocal is not true. Many great teachers never achieve the lifestyle. As we cannot attain the lifestyle without His help, teach as you grow seeking His guidance in all things - (Luke 9:62).

1.12.5 Successful managers understand humility - Remember to serve each other in love and humility, teaching from the same posture - (Acts 20:19, 1 Peter 5:5).

1.12.6 Successful managers rely on versatility - This is where the tools of the trade diversify. Everyone's calling is to teach His commandments, but everyone's method can differ - (2 Timothy 2:21).

1.12.7 Successful managers steer others towards the light - Once we were darkness, but we cannot be of use to the Kingdom, while we dwell in darkness. Here is one of God's mercy at work. Even those that fall, walk away and or stray can teach what he commanded. Ask yourself, as a manager; is it worse to have an employee that does not believe what they teach, or one who will not teach what they believe? Unlike the parable of the ten talents, of you will not partake in the kingdom, you can still help build. How many parents that are not believers, still mandate or bring their kids to church. This is preferable to the believers and the unbelievers that decide not to encourage their children to a better way of life; is it not? - (Luke16:8).

1.12.8 Successful managers utilize effective communication - Teach clear simple lessons. Jesus' use of parables is the method He felt best. Small words and precept upon precept, like Lego builds an entire Kingdom. Like Lego, the shapes and colors are designed to make a particular thing. They must fit otherwise; however, the picture will not match the one on the box - (Ephesians 4:29).

1.12.9 Successful managers act strategically - Each lesson taught is supposed to line up to John 1:3. So as we teach we each should adhere to the strictest parameters of truth and integrity. Our lesson cannot go against His Commandments in anyway; they can however completely overshadow the teachings of and reputations of men. God's managers have no responsibility to hide the lies of another men, of spread their lies, no matter if it is doctrine, or tradition. We answer to Him, and alone He warns to fear him that destroys the body and the soul - (Colossians 1:28).

1.12.10 Successful managers manage self - Control yourself and God will not have to. Teach the truth and God will not have to correct us more than necessary - (2 Peter 1:5-7).

1.12.11 Successful managers create set clear goals and insist on achieving them - Commonly known as a Vision, men mistake their setting benchmarks as a new vision of God. He has no vision other than those things set forth in His Bible. Benchmarks however, change all the time, as His people stray and or get lost - (Daniel 6:26).

1.12.12 Successful managers manage complexity - Take the deep things of God and make smaller meals. Like it is with leftovers, the portion is the only thing that may change but the contents the same. If you add or make goulash you have changed the meal. If you change the meal, the nutritional value changes as well. Additives and preservatives may make the food last longer, but they do little if anything to make the meal healthier. - (Exodus 18:16).

1.12.13 Successful managers foster creativity and innovation - Encourage our people to use all their skills to spread His words. Sing, movies, books, poems, cook, paint, dance; any tool to further the building of the Kingdom wall - (Philippians 6:1).

1.12.14 Successful managers promote teamwork - All tools work for the kingdom. All stewards that do not realize they are all working on the same project, are in the way (Matthew 3:30). Take the tools, and get up off the wall, for you are not adding to the Kingdom, or your own future - (Ephesians 4:29).

1.12.15 Successful managers create lasting relationships - Ministry friends make bonds for life. Everyone remembers kindness and warmth; consequently, of you work in the kingdom and no one likes you might be the problem. Pray for each other, serve each other, love each other, by this all me will know we are His disciples - (Amos 3:3).

1.12.16 Successful managers learn agility - Do not be Pharisaical or Sanhedral. Knowledge is not king, He is. HOWEVER, DO NOT FALL PRAY to a lie of the enemy. We cannot mimic the world to sell the gospel (Romans 3:2). Penicillin is never market as Gummi bears, yet it does a world of good. If we must change, modernize, or make the gospel politically correct; we do not understand the word. How can we make good palatable to evil? The result has been and always will be that darkness creeps into our kingdom under the guise of the modern church (Roman 8:11).

1.13
THE WARNING TO TEACHERS

"**My hand will be against the prophets who see false visions and utter lying divinations. They will not belong to the council of my people or be listed in the records of Israel, nor will they enter the land of Israel. Then you will know that I am the Sovereign Lord**," (Ezekiel 13:9).

Brothers and sisters, the book of James admonishes us to be thoughtful about teaching and moving into the calling of teaching in any of its forms, for teachers come under a harsher judgment. This does not mean that there is a separate set of rules or commandments for teacher, it just means that the Owner of the flock while overlooking the flaws of the sheep; allows little room if any for shepherds to squander, mislead, abandon, fleece, or deceive His flock (Jeremiah 23:1).

Be ye not deceived, while you are free to go to hell on your own, it is the Fathers pleasure than none perish, and His measure that no one taken from Him[19]. It makes sense that He who give His life to save will not sit idly by while those He died to redeem are lead back into bondage.

If you respond to the call, aspire to excel in the management of your presentation. Be prepared, by studying what He said. Be prepared to answer questions, by doing extra reading on words and themes promoted by the Master. Master the craft, the single most important thing you will do with your life is leads souls to salvation; the fruit of our teaching is Life, and they that win souls are wise.

In thy getting, get understand the Bible says, then understand the call to mastery, is the call to servanthood. My Blackbelt allows me to teach others, and bring them up to where I am. I love promoting under-belts. I know they cannot overshadow or take my black belt, therefore I do not fear them. In the same manner I have learned to enjoy teaching Kingdom promises and helping make more teachers. They cannot take my calling; therefore, I need not fear them, and we are not competition.

Get a flock you can manage and master managing your own flock; there are enough sheep to mandate teacher making long into the future. Let the envy and pride fall away, by making His Kingdom the priority, in turn; you may develop material wealth. If; however, the latter is the former, then what have you to do with Him, more importantly - what will He have to do with you? I think He tells you what He is going to do with those who betray their calling as a teacher; they are accursed[20].

1.14 WARNINGS ABOUT TEACHERS

"**For the time will come when people will not put up with sound doctrine. Instead, to suit their own desires, they will gather around them a great number of teachers to say what their itching ears want to hear. They will turn their ears away from the truth and turn aside to myths**." (2 Timothy 4:3-4).

God in His infinite wisdom prepares His word to account for the lies within the church. The reason for this is simple, a corrupt people invariably produce corrupt ministers and officers in the church. N.B., I did not say of the church, because the Church does not produce corruption of any kind. As with any fruitful marriage, the husband and wife have children. In this case, the husband paid the price to remove the stain of His bride and presented her without spot or blemish. Only spotless fruit comes from Christian marriage. Therefore, in John 8:44, He claims we are like our father the Devil, confirming why He took it upon Himself to warn the flock about teachers - because they do not work for or worth Him.

The Scriptures contain;
1. #14 warnings against False Teachings[21]
2. #7 warnings against False Prophets[22]
3. #3 warnings about False Teachings[23]

As we think about the warnings about teachers and teachings we want to look at somethings we need to be able to discern for our students or as a student from our teachers.

1.14.1 **Where does the message come from?** - Is this teaching, based on scripture or opinion? This make all the difference I the world. Anything other than scripture us accursed. Opinion falls into the category of other than scripture, so keep it to yourself. We teach opinion at our own peril. Anything other than scripture, is an insidious ploy from the devil, designed to deter the hearers from the truth of the Gospel.

1.14.2 **What is the substance of the message?** - When we deliver the entire message, what is the point of the message. Is the message designed to get the hearer to the truth of Jesus Christ or further into the darkness we serve? Is the meat of the message salvation or damnation?

1.14.3 **In what position will the message leave hearers**? - Is the content of the message in keeping with perfecting the saints.

1.14.4 **What kind of people does the message produce?** - The fruit of the Spirit yields truth and righteous?

1.14.5 **Why should people listen to the message?** - Should we listen to the message because if improves our relationship with God? Does the message improve our everyday lives? Does the message bring us closer to the truth?

1.14.6 What result does the message have in people's lives? - What effect does this message have on our relationship with God? What effect does this message have on our everyday lives? After the message bring us closer to the truth?

1.14.7 Where does the message ultimately lead hearers? - Jesus said I am the way the truth and the Life, no one come through the Father but thorough me. Therefore, what we teach either leads people to or away from Jesus there is no in between. Just like there is no in between or unclarity in Matthew 18:6, "**But whoso shall offend (mislead) one of these little ones which believe in me, it were better for him that a millstone were hanged about his neck, and that he were drowned in the depth of the sea**."

DO NOT BE DECEIVED, THE LORD OF THE
HARVEST WILL AND DOES NOT FORGET

1.15
THE PURPOSE OF CREDENTIALS[24]

The foundation of credentials indicates medicine as the primary specialty. However, many stories have hidden in them titles which when looked at more closely are credentials in nature. As far back as 1110 BC[25], the ancient Persian cult of Zoraster determined a process for credentialing physicians. As medicine improved, and science begin to highlight that medicine needed rules, credentialing developed to ensure that physicians are capable and qualified to perform the task.

In the Bible, Chief, Head, First, Primary, Scribe, Pharisee, Sadducee, and High, all indicated rank achieved via apprenticeship or tutelage and recognize as expertise. If these credentials were not important, the priest would not have pressed Jesus for His credentials, and the disciples would not have questioned Jesus about rank in the Kingdom.

In respected fields, and when competency is required we credential. As a result, of the demand for credentials, counterfeiting has become a problem. Since there is much at stake frauds constantly devise ways to counterfeit credentials, and companies have to device countermeasure to verify. Here are few examples of credentials;

1. **Diplomatic Credentials** - A letter of credence is a document that ambassadors, diplomats, chargés d'affaires carry to detail diplomatic rank. It also contains a request that full credibility be given to his official statements.

2. **Medical Credentials** - Detail all training, and permissions granted a medical doctor, physician assistant or nurse practitioner at every institution at which he or she has worked in the past. Most Medical credentials also require continuing

education to ensure current and verifiable knowledge.

3. **Operator license** - Received after successful training and/or examination.

4. **Academic and professional credentials** - Attest knowledge, skills, and ability necessary to practice an occupation competently.

    I assembled this section for one purpose, because during the assemblage of the information for this resource I found documentation, verification, and education of Apostles and Prophets scant.
    There exisits ample documentation about Apostles and Prophets and their duties pertaining to the scriptures, but their actual qualifications are not always straightforward.
    Even more disturbing, alarming, is the fact that modern literature has straight documentation for Pastors, Elders, Deacons and Evangelists but no such formatting is straight forward. In terms of Apostles and Prophets, there is ample information as to how to test them and some magic and wizard stories about how to verify prophecy, but nothing that looks remotely credential worthy.

The lack of formal requisites lends itself to a horrific question; Does the church not care about credentialing these ministry positions, or do people choose these ministry positions chosen because they cannot be credentialled?

I believe the latter is the reason. There is no reason to be a pastor of a sedentary church body and proport to be an Apostle or Prophet. The title does not give the authority, the functions do.

God credentialled Jeremiah, before his birth. Jeremiah DID NOT SEEK GOD'S HAND AFTER CLAIMING THE TITLE, "**Before I formed thee in the belly I knew thee; and before thou camest forth out of the womb I sanctified thee, and I ordained thee a prophet unto the nations. Then said I, Ah, Lord GOD! behold, I cannot speak: for I am a child. But the Lord said unto me, 'Say not, I am a child: for thou shalt go to all that I shall send thee, and whatsoever I command thee thou shalt speak. Be not afraid of their faces: for I am with thee to deliver thee,' saith the Lord.**

Then the Lord put forth his hand and touched my mouth. And the Lord said unto me, 'Behold, I have put my words in thy mouth' (Jeremiah 1:5-9)".

There is no reason to believe this process has changed, the gifts and anointing may be without repentance, but they still came from God and therefore are verifiable by His Spirit. We must therefore rely even more heavily on the Elders filled with the Spirit to aid in the discernment and monitoring of modern Apostles and Prophets.

This resource recommends when evaluating persons (onboarding) consider Apostles and Prophets a modular advancement. In other words, we should evaluate these positions using primary vocational aptitude as well as traits and discernment i.e. Pastor and Prophet etc. The person that claims to be an apostle or prophet should show fluence at a credentialed position.

The Medical specialist serves as a resident in an established field before they are allowed and credentialed as a specialist. The church must employ similar criterion, lest we constantly subject sheep to dangerous sprits and teachings.

1.16
CAIAPHASTICS©26

"**For there is no respect of persons with God**" (Romans 2:11).

"**At that time the disciples came to Jesus asked, 'Who, then, is the the greatest in the kingdom of heaven?' and said, Verily I say unto you, except ye be converted, and become as little children ye shall not enter into the Kingdom of Heaven**" (Matthew 18:1&3).

All scriptures are true, and the converse is always true as well. Therefore, we must also understand that if God is no respecter of person, He also does is not concerned with our impression of rank in the Kingdom.

Caiaphas was a chief priest, and he held rank. Because of his rank people obeyed him and feared him. This man however, paid to have Jesus' betrayed and His body moved, because he knew the Jesus out ranked him.

Since we did not redeem anyone and baptize them in our blood, they need not jump at our command, nor fear us. Jesus death saved them (sheep) from us (teachers) as well.

If God watched them scourge Jesus do you really think He holds to the Old Testament rules about hierarchy in the Temple. More importantly, if we teach that the Lord of the Harvest[27] finds distaste in poor treatment of clergy - how do we think He feels about the Clerical abuses of His people.

Another Caiaphastic trait to be leery of; Leaders that swear God called them and gave them a title, but they cannot tell you what the duties and/or responsibilities of that calling. How sad, a servant called by the Most High, that is more interested in claiming the title, than learning the job and doing it well. No matter what our call is, the proper response is to ascertain what exactly we have been called to, train for that mission, and adapt tools and skills which are mission specific. Even US Navy SEALs train to be the best on Sea, Air and Land; at what their job description demands. They do not change tires or ring bells, during the Christmas holidays.

2.0 BECOMING A MORE EFFECTIVE TEACHER

"Further, because Shepard was wise, he still taught the people knowledge. Yes, he pondered, sought out, and set in order many proverbs. The preacher sought to find out acceptable words, and that which was written blamelessly, words of truth. The words of the wise are like goads; and like nails well fastened are words from the masters of assemblies, which are given from one shepherd. Furthermore, my son, be admonished: of making many books there is no end; and much study is a weariness of the flesh." (Ecclesiastes 3:9-11).

2.0
A DEFINITION OF TEACHER

Our definition of a teacher is; **a person that either exemplifies, edifies or instructs on a certain place or thing.** A Teacher is a painter. The painter does not create the art they paint they simply paint images. A teacher therefore simply explains how to connect the tidbits we call knowledge into a functioning flow called wisdom.

2.1 WHAT A LESSON SHOULD ENTAIL

A lesson should contain the method(s) for connecting these dots. Language is the best example of this principle. From 26 letters (dots) we create hundreds of thousands of words. None of these words have any innate meaning, they only mean what we agree that they mean. Language is a Masterpiece.

I hold a Black belt in Martial arts, which means the Eastern Wado Ryu Federation considers me to have mastered the craft. The purpose of mastering the art was not hold the information secret but to prepare myself to answer all the possible questions the under belts may have. Proficiency in a discipline is often required, but those without this mastery hold us in esteem. The converse is what our lessons should entail. The knowledge we obtain is to serve them not to manipulate or lord over them.

2.2 WHAT MAKES AN EFFECTIVE TEACHER?

Please take time to look at list and tick of which elements you lack and how you plan to upgrade your arsenal.

2.2.1 Wisdom
- [ ] Knowledge
- [ ] Competency
- [ ] Fluency of topic and related topics

2.2.2 Knowledge
- [ ] Knowledge of teaching
- [ ] The characteristics of knowledge
- [ ] Interesting

- [ ] Informative
- [ ] Truthful
- [ ] Ever training

2.2.3 Pondering proverbs
- [ ] Considering existing wisdom
- [ ] Understanding existing wisdom

2.2.4 Arranging proverbs
- [ ] Conforming to existing wisdom
- [ ] Interpolating new wisdom

2.2.5 Use of acceptable words
- [ ] Not using profanity
- [ ] Not intimidating
- [ ] Truthful
- [ ] Not politically correct

2.2.6 Inoffensive
- [ ] Not opinionated
- [ ] Know when and where to use provocative words
- [ ] Relate words of truth

2.2.7 Words of truth
- [ ] Always teach the truth and not opinion
- [ ] If you only have opinion and rhetoric it is not teaching, it is conditioning

2.2.8 Simple
- [ ] LCS…Lowest common student
- [ ] Teach to the lowest level of the audience
- [ ] Teach at a speed so that no one is confused

- [ ] Teach so that no one is left behind

2.2.9 Increasing knowledge
- [ ] Must increase the level of knowledge
- [ ] Must modify the level of understanding
- [ ] Must increase awareness
- [ ] Must increase student horizons and scope of thought

2.2.11 Bring student closer to the truth
- [ ] The truth convicts
- [ ] A lesson that tries to sway or persuade is argumentative not informative
- [ ] An Apostle's job is to teach a person how to think not what to think
- [ ] This is the difference between intelligence and education
- [ ] Education is more akin to indoctrination - teaching is more like exposure

2.2.11 Release the student's minds to grow
- [ ] Free the student's minds to grow
- [ ] Teach them how to formulate a thought

2.2.3 Use as a building block
- [ ] Learn how to think
- [ ] Learn how to build on these blocks
- [ ] Wisdom comes from above

2.3 NECESSARY TOOLS FOR A TEACHER

2.3.1 Poling
☐ Always poll the audience with questions, or by opening the floor with questions. This allows for more feedback and gets them involved.

2.3.2 Anime
☐ Despite what type style you use anime is necessary
☐ Can be the use of color
☐ Can be the use of jokes
☐ Can be the use of voice inflection
☐ Can be the use or movement

2.3.3 Fluence
☐ You must learn your topic intimately
☐ There is nothing more pathetic than a Teacher that cannot answer questions

2.3.4 Pliability
☐ You must be able to answer questions handle criticism or explain supporting concepts.

2.3.5 Use of color[28]
☐ Greens are great for counseling
☐ Blue is calming
☐ Yellow for creativity
☐ Gentle energy yellows for languages and creative pursuits

- ☐ Oranges & Peach tones for drama and media
- ☐ Variety is important as is the amount of variety. Too little can set up patterns of boredom & introversion. Too much can strain the mind with overstimulation

3.0 BECOMING A MORE EFFECTIVE PASTOR

"Keep watch over yourselves and all the flock of which the Holy Spirit has made you overseers. Be shepherds of the church of God, which He bought with His own blood" - (Acts 20:28).

3.0
A DEFINITION OF PASTOR

Our definition of a Pastor derives from the Latin noun pastor which means 'shepherd' and relates to the Latin verb ☐☐ ☐☐☐☐ - 'to lead to pasture, set to grazing, cause to eat'. The term is similar to the New Testament but does not indicate singular function of preaching. All pastors can minister/preach, but all ministers can be pastors.

3.1 TYPICAL PASTORAL DUTIES

- ☐ Preaching and teaching: The Pastor is the primary speaker for worship services.

- ☐ The Pastor also will provide leadership in planning and executing the Adult Education programs and other programs in discipleship and ministry training, in coordination with other ordained and lay leaders.

- ☐ Strategic leadership and planning: Responsible for strategic planning and staff coordination in the execution of the church's purpose.

- ☐ The Pastor will define strategic goals and benchmarks as a key leader among staff and elders and implement the plan by coordinating/leading weekly staff meetings and other activities to clarify and execute goals and objectives, monitoring the spiritual pulse of the congregation through review and accountability, ensuring staffing, facilities and programs are effectively aligned to meet strategic goals.

- ☐ Staff supervision and development: The Pastor serves as director to ordained and lay staff and lay volunteers, and leads, evaluates, and mentors existing staff in their respective areas of ministry

- ☐ Maintaining efficient and effective lines of communication between the staff and elders.

☐ Spiritual Administration: The Pastor oversees and executes the administration of the church through proper staff and lay leadership teams, and ensures the completion of ministry, business, facility, and logistical support functions through staff and lay volunteers.

☐ Oversee the Pastoral needs of the congregation and, as necessary, share with other ordained and lay ministers in hospital visitation, home visits, counseling, marriages, and funerals.

☐ Participate in development of and adherence to church policies and procedures.

3.2
WHAT A PASTORAL LESSON SHOULD ENTAIL

Remembering that the Sunday sermon is the Emergency Room for all churches and all lives, the sermon should be general, simple, and useful. Here is a list of at least 13 things all sermons should cover.

3.2.1 ☐ Scripture clarity - What is the main point of my text[29]? An effective sermon should ensure your text supports the truth, not your sermon

3.2.2 ☐ Sermon clarity - What is the main point of my sermon? Ensure that your sermon is based on and reinforces the truth, not opinion

3.2.3 ☐ Sermon purpose - What is the motivation behind the sermon? All sermons should conform to the Triune Learning System® which is all about God
- The Lesson - What we see in Christ and what we should emulate
- The Teacher - What we are told by Christ and what we should teacher others
- The Student - What we learn from Christ and or how to apply His words to our lives

3.2.4 ☐ What is at stake - What if the truths of this passage are not obeyed? Use of the prophetic warnings and Gods judgements against the church

3.2.5 ☐ Supporting Documentation for the Sermon - Use simple clear, gripping illustrations and support to make the lesson both understandable and memorable

3.2.6 ☐ What stories, examples, illustrations, and creative elements will help people see, feel, and respond to the sermon? - Use texts and parables which illustrate application of the sermon contents

3.2.7 ☐ How should the sermon end? - Does not always have to end with invitation make the sermon responsive to the Spirit and be flexible

3.2.8 ☐ Can I make the sermon shorter? - 25 minutes is a long speech, try not to go long, or break it up with illustrations and stories

3.2.9 ☐ If I preached my sermon to Jesus one-on-one, would he say that my life embodied this message? - Bring God to life via the sermon

3.2.10 ☐ Is there an equal emphasis on the word and the spirit? - During the sermon, people should encounter God's Word and God's Spirit. Bring the entire experience to life.

3.2.11 ☐ Is this sermon rooted in love? - I want people to feel God's love and be drawn to Him through the sermon.

3.2.12 ☐ Will I trust the outcome to God? - God will make the difference; the sermon should invite God into the church and our lives. We just deliver the sermon; God delivers the souls.

3.3
WHAT MAKES AN EFFECTIVE PASTOR?

In each of these sections, we offer a list of attributes compiled to improve the conveyance of information and the maturation of the audience. A Pastor like any teach has room to grow, and ample time to practice. But the imperative to improve must be to please God, not ambition. Please take time to look at list and tick of which elements you lack and how you plan to upgrade your arsenal.

3.3.1 **Wisdom**
- ☐ Knowledge
- ☐ Competency
- ☐ Fluency of topic and related topics

3.3.2 **Knowledge**
- ☐ Knowledge of teaching
- ☐ The characteristics of knowledge
- ☐ Interesting
- ☐ Informative
- ☐ Truthful
- ☐ Ever training

3.3.3 **Pondering proverbs**
- ☐ Considering existing wisdom
- ☐ Understanding existing wisdom

3.3.4 **Arranging proverbs**
- ☐ Conforming to existing wisdom
- ☐ Interpolating new wisdom

3.3.5 **Use of acceptable words**
- ☐ Not using profanity

_____
_____
_____
_____
_____
_____
_____
_____
_____
_____
_____
_____
_____
_____
_____
_____
_____
_____

- [ ] Not intimidating
- [ ] Truthful
- [ ] Not politically correct

3.3.6 Inoffensive
- [ ] Not opinionated
- [ ] Relate words of truth
- [ ] Know when and where to use provocative words

3.3.7 Words of truth
- [ ] Always teach the truth and not opinion
- [ ] If you only have opinion and rhetoric it is not teaching, it is conditioning

3.3.8 Simple
- [ ] LCS…Lowest common student
- [ ] Teach to the lowest level of the congregation
- [ ] Teach at a speed so that no one is confused
- [ ] Teach so that no one is left behind

3.3.9 Increasing knowledge
- [ ] Must increase the level of knowledge
- [ ] Must modify the level of understanding
- [ ] Must increase awareness
- [ ] Must increase congregation's horizons and scope of thought

3.3.10 **Bring student closer to the truth**
- [ ] The truth convicts
- [ ] A lesson that tries to sway or persuade is argumentative not informative
- [ ] A pastor's job is to teach a person how to listen to God
- [ ] This is the difference between intelligence and education
- [ ] Education is akin to indoctrination - teaching more like exposure

3.3.11 **Release the students mind to grow**
- [ ] Free the congregation's minds to grow
- [ ] Teach them how to study the word of God

3.3.12 **Use as a building block**
- [ ] Learn how to study
- [ ] Learn how to build on these blocks

3.4
THE NECESSARY TOOLS FOR A PASTOR[30]

3.4.1 ☐ No more pretending to be perfect - Share your mistakes it gives others the courage to be honest about theirs and not to be judgmental.

3.4.2 ☐ Stop emotionally and spiritually abusing ministry staff - They work with you not for you (James 5:1-5).

3.4.3 ☐ Stop hiding secret addictions - Eventually it will be uncovered or brought to the surface. Either way the lie damages your witness and efficacy.

3.4.4 ☐ Spend more time with God - A pastor's first duty is to develop and maintain a strong relationship with God.

3.4.5 ☐ Stop talking about your 'smoking hot wife' - Praise her Godly character.

3.4.6 ☐ Remember God is the reason for our church's success - We just plant, another gives the increase.

3.4.7 ☐ Stop comparing yourself to other pastors - Become last and that's how God says we become first.

3.4.8 ☐ Stop sacrificing your family in the name of doing 'ministry' - We must shepherd at home first and steward at home lest we risk losing our home tending to another man's flock.

3.4.9 ☐ Reading business books more than your bible - Stewardship is God's idea, the world learned it from him. We must study his will and ways about his business.

3.4.10 ☐ Stop wasting the church's tithe money on wasteful expenses - Stop stealing gods money from his people. The people and the law might not find out, but God will not.

3.4.11 ☐ Stop pointless mission trips - We pass lost souls every day. With technology, and discipleship expensive trips may be needless.

3.4.12 ☐ Stop saying your church is going to 'reach the world' - Reaching the world is for the universal church, encourage working together, not separation. This is also arrogant presumption, for it gives the connotation that God speaks only to you.

3.4.13 ☐ Preach only the bible - Teach only what Jesus commanded, His words are life.

3.4.14 ☐ Eliminate selfish service - Stop being a publican and wearing your Ephod for all to see. Do what you do for God, never for publicity.

3.5 QUESTIONNAIRE FOR PASTORAL CANDIDATE[31]

These questions compromise a list of basic areas needing coverage from every pastoral candidate, as they cover the basic duties and areas of knowledge. Without a basic fluence in these areas, the candidate will damage their flock and also their relationship with God.

3.5.1   List your hobbies and any other areas of interest apart from ministry.
3.5.2   Describe how you came into a relationship with Christ.
3.5.3   Describe your call to the ministry and what motivates you to stay in ministry.
3.5.4   Describe your day-to-day spiritual life.
3.5.5   How do you get spiritually refreshed?
3.5.6   Have you ever been treated for depression?
3.5.7   What role does personal evangelism play in your life?
3.5.8   What steps do you follow to lead someone to Christ?
3.5.9   Describe the role of accountability for a pastor and how that has been a part of your life.
3.5.10 Please share how you came to know and follow Jesus Christ.
3.5.11 How long have you been a believer?
3.5.12 How are you strengthening and growing your relationship with the Lord?
3.5.13 What role does discipleship play in your life?
3.5.14 What do you do to support your health?
3.5.15 What do you do for fun?
3.5.16 How do you balance your life between family and ministry?
3.5.17 How is your wife/husband involved in ministry?
3.5.18 How do the pressures of the ministry and expectations of the congregation affect your family? How have you responded in the past?
3.5.19 How do you keep a quality relationship with your wife/husband?
3.5.20 How does your family feel about the possibility of your ministry move?
3.5.21 How do you function as the spiritual leader of your family?
3.5.22 What would you name as your passion in ministry?

3.5.23 What is the most enjoyable part of your current ministry position?
3.5.24 Describe your spiritual gifts and how the Lord uses them in ministry.
3.5.25 In what areas of ministry do you feel most experienced and competent?
3.5.26 What role do you see evangelism playing in a believer's life?
3.5.27 How do you define "Discipleship"?
3.5.28 Describe any earlier experience in deciding long-range goals and other types of planning activities.
3.5.29 What do you perceive the major task of the church to be and what do you see as your role in that?
3.5.30 What role do you see the Lay leadership having in the local church?
3.5.31 What would be your desired method of church government?
3.5.32 What are your views on the relationship between: the staff, the board of elders, and the board of deacons?
3.5.33 How do you identify the need for and go about developing a new area of ministry?
3.5.34 How do you supervise, motivate and develop staff, interns and lay leaders?
3.5.35 How do you define a leadership team?
3.5.36 What personality type do you best work with and what type do you struggle with?
3.5.37 What type of staff environment do you function in most effectively?
3.5.38 How do you help change?
3.5.39 How would you address an unexpected budget shortfall?
3.5.40 What do you feel are the strengths and weaknesses of short term mission trips? Long term vocational missions?
3.5.41 What have you seen are some of the trends in missions?
3.5.42 What role do you see small groups fulfilling in the church?
3.5.43 What experiences do you have in small groups?
3.5.44 How important is the children's ministry to a growing and dynamic church?
3.5.45 How important is a youth ministry to a growing and dynamic church?
3.5.46 How important is a single adult ministry to a growing and dynamic church?
3.5.47 Describe your philosophy of ministry for equipping the body.
3.5.48 What experience do you have in leading a pastoral staff team?
3.5.49 What do you see as the primary purpose for the Sunday morning services?
3.5.50 Describe your philosophy of worship.

3.5.51 What is your opinion on non-traditional forms of worship (e.g., Theatrical productions, multi-media presentations, etc.)?
3.5.52 What is your view of pastoral counseling?
3.5.53 How have you handled pastoral counseling in the past?
3.5.54 How much time (weekly) have you carved out of your schedule for counseling
3.5.55 Are there any points in our doctrinal statement that you would not or could not affirm?
3.5.56 What is you view of the baptism and filling of the Holy Spirit?
3.5.57 How would you advise a person who comes to you and says he or she wants a divorce?
3.5.58 What is your view of abortion?
3.5.59 What is your view of women in the church?
3.5.60 What is your position on the recent movement in churches to become "Seeker Sensitive" or "Seeker Driven"?
3.5.61 Please share how you came to know and follow Jesus Christ.
3.5.62 How long have you been a believer?

_____
_____
_____
_____
_____
_____
_____
_____
_____
_____
_____
_____
_____
_____
_____
_____

4.0 BECOMING A MORE EFFECTIVE PROPHET

"I will raise them up a Prophet from among their brethren, like unto thee, and will put my words in his mouth; and he shall speak unto them all that I shall command him. And it shall come to pass, that whosoever will not hearken unto my words which he shall speak in my name, I will require it of him. But the prophet, which shall presume to speak a word in my name, which I have not commanded him to speak, or that shall speak in the name of other gods, even that prophet shall die. And if thou say in thine heart, how shall we know the word which the Lord hath not spoken? When a prophet speaketh in the name of the Lord, if the thing follow not, nor come to pass, that is the thing which the Lord hath not spoken, but the prophet hath spoken it presumptuously: thou shalt not be afraid of him," - (Deuteronomy 18:18-22).

4.0
A DEFINITION OF PROPHET

Our definition of a Prophet is; a person that either exemplifies, edifies the church, relays God's judgements, or instructs on a certain place or future thing by direct commission of God. He is not a diviner or a frequenter of familiar spirits. Most importantly, He does not make predictions, He relays the decrees of God.

4.1 **TYPICAL DUTIES OF A PROPHET**

- [ ] Correction and admonishment
- [ ] Warns of judgement
- [ ] Directs
- [ ] Encourages
- [ ] Intercedes
- [ ] Teaches
- [ ] Counsels
- [ ] Tells the church to respond to the Words of God
- [ ] Edifies the church
- [ ] Prayer
- [ ] Mediates and intercedes
- [ ] Encouragement
- [ ] Calls to repentance
- [ ] Calls to practical holiness
- [ ] Interpreting dreams and visions
- [ ] Exposing false leadership
- [ ] Warns of danger
- [ ] Interpreting the signs of the times
- [ ] Testing of prophecy
- [ ] Watches out for the church
- [ ] Invites God's action
- [ ] Explain theology
- [ ] Healing the sick
- [ ] Appoints and anoints leaders
- [ ] Advising leadership; within and outside the church
- [ ] Combat false teacher and teaching

4.2 **PERSONALITY TRAITS OF PROPHETS**[32]

- ☐ Expressive
- ☐ Judgmental
- ☐ Alertness
- ☐ Brutally honest
- ☐ Crude
- ☐ Justice seeker
- ☐ Unforgiving
- ☐ Dedicated
- ☐ Determined
- ☐ Stubborn
- ☐ Loyal
- ☐ Zealous

4.3
A WARNING ABOUT PROPHETS, PROPHECY AND FAMILIAR SPIRITS

"The prophets prophesy falsely, and the priests bear rule by their means; and my people love to have it so: and what will ye do in the end thereof?" - (Jeremiah 5:31).

Personal prophecy (Words of Knowledge or Wisdom) is NOT THE SAME GIFT AS PROPHECY. We must treat Word of Knowledge[33] with caution. God's prophetic Word is **not** usually personally directive. Also, since word of Knowledge does not edify the church (necessarily), there is no reason to believe it would happen in public forum, it can be personal. Personal only in so much as they are not to edify the entre church, they still cannot tell you where to find lost keys and most certainly do not talk to the dead[34].

Hearers must try the spirit of the message to differentiate it from familiar spirits[35]. Consequently, it is dangerous to make life changing decisions on the basis of a Prophets may confirm something God already said, but this occurs generally because the person has not learnt God's voice or is ignoring God's voice.

4.2.1 #51 WARNINGS ABOUT FAMILIAR SPIRITS[36]

Before we look together at the #51 warnings in the scriptures against fortune tellers, witchcraft, wizards, and diviners (necromancers) let us take a moment to pause and look at the three most famous Wizards in the Bible. According to the story found in Matthew 2:1-16, the three men present at the Birth. As ourselves why they were present? The answer comes from Revelations 13 and also is part of the warnings against false hoods.

According to Strong's the Greek word used for the three Kings is *magus* Defined as;

1. *The name given by the Babylonians (Chaldeans), Medes, Persians, and others, to the wise men, teachers, priests, physicians, astrologers, seers, interpreters of dreams, augers, soothsayers, sorcerers etc.*

2. *The oriental wise men (astrologers) who, having discovered by the rising of a remarkable star that the Messiah had just been born, came to Jerusalem to worship him*

3. *A false prophet and sorcerer*

From Revelations 13:1 and 11 we find the beasts sent by Satan have powers and divinations. Named among them in this passage is NOT prophecy, although they do teach. What we find is that the Magus (Wise Men) represented the underworld, the Dark Arts later called *magic*. But they came to see the One that was not false, not a wizard, not a magician, not a diviner, not a familiar spirit, or an enchanter; but instead I AM, the Creator of all things. They were also there to prove that He was NOT the Antichrist. Who better to identify the genuine article than those who practice against Him.

- Leviticus 19:31 - **"Do not turn to mediums or wizard; do not seek them out, and so make yourselves unclean by them: I am the Lord your God."**

- Leviticus 20:6 - **"If a person turns to mediums and wizard, whoring after them, I will set my face against that person and will cut him off from among his people."**

- Leviticus 20:27 - **"A man or a woman who is a medium or a wizard shall surely be put to death. They shall be stoned with stones; their blood shall be upon them."**

- Leviticus 19:26 - **"You shall not eat any flesh with the blood in it. You shall not interpret omens or tell fortunes."**

- Isaiah 8:19 - **And when they say to you, "Inquire of the mediums and the wizard who chirp and mutter," should not a people inquire of their God? Should they inquire of the dead-on behalf of the living."**

- Isaiah 29:4 - **"And you will be brought low; from the earth you shall speak, and from the dust your speech will be**

- bowed down; your voice shall come from the ground like the voice of a ghost, and from the dust your speech shall whisper."

- Isaiah 19:3 - **"And the spirit of the Egyptians within them will be emptied out, and I will confound their counsel; and they will inquire of the idols and the sorcerers, and the mediums and the wizard;**

- 2 Chronicles 33:6 - **"And he burned his sons as an offering in the Valley of the Son of Hinnom, and used fortune-telling and omens and sorcery, and dealt with mediums and with wizard. He did much evil in the sight of the Lord, provoking him to anger."**

- 1 Chronicles 10:13 - **"So Saul died for his breach of faith. He broke faith with the L**ORD** in that he did not keep the command of the Lord, and also consulted a medium, seeking guidance."**

- Kings 21:6 - **"And he burned his son as an offering and used fortune-telling and omens and dealt with mediums and with wizard. He did much evil in the sight of the Lord, provoking him to anger."**

- 2 Kings 23:24 - **"Moreover, Josiah put away the mediums and the wizard and the household gods and the idols and all the abominations that were seen in the land of Judah and in Jerusalem, that he might establish the words of the law that were written in the book that Hilkiah the priest found in the house of the Lord."**

- 2 Kings 9:22 - **"And when Joram saw Jehu, he said, "Is it peace, Jehu?" He answered, "What peace can there be, so long as the whorings and the sorceries of your mother Jezebel are so many?"**

- 2 Kings 17:17 - **"And they burned their sons and their daughters as offerings and used divination and omens and sold themselves to do evil in the sight of the L**ORD**, provoking him to anger."**

- Deuteronomy 18:10 - **"There shall not be found among you anyone who burns his son or his daughter as an offering, anyone who practices divination or tells fortunes or interprets omens, or a sorcerer."**

- Deuteronomy 18:11 - **"Or a charmer or a medium or a wizard or one who inquires of the dead,"**

- Deuteronomy 18:14 - **"For these nations, which you are about to dispossess, listen to fortune-tellers and to diviners. But as for you, the Lord your God has not allowed you to do this."**

- Deuteronomy 18:10-3 - **"There shall not be found among you anyone who burns his son or his daughter as an offering, anyone who practices divination or tells fortunes or interprets omens, or a sorcerer or a charmer or a medium or a wizard or one who inquires of the dead, for whoever does these things is an abomination to the Lord. And because of these abominations the Lord your God is driving them out before you."**

- Deuteronomy 18:11-3 - **"Or a charmer or a medium or a wizard or one who inquires of the dead, for whoever does these things is an abomination to the Lord. And because of these abominations the Lord your God is driving them out before you."**

- Deuteronomy 18:10-11 - **"There shall not be found among you anyone who burns his son or his daughter as an offering, anyone who practices divination or tells fortunes or interprets omens, or a sorcerer or a charmer or a medium or a wizard or one who inquires of the dead,"**

- Deuteronomy 18:9-3 - **"When you come into the land that the Lord your God is giving you, you shall not learn to follow the abominable practices of those nations. There shall not be found among you anyone who burns his son or his daughter as an offering, anyone who practices divination or tells fortunes or interprets omens, or a sorcerer or a charmer or a medium or a wizard or one who inquires of the dead, for whoever does these things is an abomination to the Lord. And because of these abominations the Lord your God is driving them out before you."**

- Deuteronomy 18:9-14 - **"When you come into the land that the Lord your God is giving you, you shall not learn to follow the abominable practices of those nations. There shall not be found among you anyone who burns his son or his daughter as an offering, anyone who practices divination or tells fortunes or interprets omens, or a sorcerer or a charmer or a medium or a wizard or one who inquires of the dead, for whoever does these things is an abomination to the Lord. And because of these abominations the Lord your God is driving them out before you. You shall be blameless before the Lord your God,"**

- 1 Samuel 28:1-9 - **"Now Samuel had died, and all Israel had mourned for him and buried him in Ramah, his own city. And Saul had put the mediums and the wizard out of the land. The Philistines assembled and came and encamped at Shunem. And Saul gathered all**

Israel, and they encamped at Gilboa. When Saul saw the army of the Philistines, he was afraid, and his heart trembled greatly. And when Saul inquired of the Lord, the LORD did not answer him, either by dreams, or by Urim, or by prophets. Then Saul said to his servants, "Seek out for me a woman who is a medium, that I may go to her and inquire of her." And his servants said to him, "Behold, there is a medium at En-dor, And Saul disguised himself, and put on other raiment, and he went, and two men with him, and they came to the woman by night: and he said, I pray thee, divine unto me by the familiar spirit, and bring me him up, whom I shall name unto thee. And the woman said unto him, Behold, thou knowest what Saul hath done, how he hath cut off those that have familiar spirits, and the wizards, out of the land: wherefore then layest thou a snare for my life, to cause me to die?"

- Daniel 2:27 - **"Daniel answered the king and said, "No wise men, enchanters, magicians, or astrologers can show to the king the mystery that the king has asked,"**

- Nahum 3:4 - **"And all for the countless whorings of the prostitute, graceful and of deadly charms, who betrays nations with her whorings, and peoples with her charms."**

- Jeremiah 1:1-19 - **"The words of Jeremiah, the son of Hilkiah, one of the priests who were in Anathoth in the land of Benjamin, to whom the word of the Lord came in the days of Josiah the son of Amon, king of Judah, in the thirteenth year of his reign. It came also in the days of Jehoiakim the son of Josiah, king of Judah, and until the end of the eleventh year of Zedekiah, the son of Josiah, king of Judah, until the captivity of Jerusalem in the fifth month. Now the word of the Lord came to me, saying, "Before I formed you in** the womb I knew you, and before you were born I consecrated you; I appointed you a prophet to the nations."

- Acts 8:9 - **"But there was a man named Simon, who had previously practiced magic in the city and amazed the people of Samaria, saying that he himself was somebody great."**

- Acts 16:16-18 - **"As we were going to the place of prayer, we were met by a slave girl who had a spirit of divination and brought her owners much gain by fortune-telling. She followed Paul and us, crying out, "These men are servants of the Highest God, who proclaim to you the way of salvation." And this she kept doing for many days. Paul, having become greatly annoyed, turned and said to the spirit, "I command you in the name of Jesus Christ to come out of her." And it came out that very hour."**

- Acts 19:19 - **"And a number of those who had practiced magic arts brought their books together and burned them in the sight of all. And they counted the value of them and found it came to fifty thousand pieces of silver."**

- Luke 16:27-31 - **"And he said, 'Then I beg you, father, to send him to my father's house for I have five brothers–so that he may warn them, lest they also come into this place of torment.' But Abraham said, 'They have Moses and the Prophets; let them hear them.' And he said, 'No, father Abraham, but if someone goes to them from the dead, they will repent.' He said to him, 'If they do not hear Moses and the Prophets, neither will they be convinced if someone should rise from the dead.'"**

- Exodus 7:11 - **"Then Pharaoh summoned the wise men and the sorcerers, and they, the magicians of Egypt, also did the same by their secret arts."**

- Micah 5:3 - **"And I will cut off sorceries from your hand, and you shall have no more tellers of fortunes;"**

- Psalm 68:1-35 - **"To the choirmaster. A Psalm of David. A Song. God shall arise, his enemies shall be scattered; and those who hate him shall flee before him! As smoke is driven away, so you shall drive them away; as wax melts before fire, so the wicked shall perish before God! But the righteous shall be glad; they shall exult before God; they shall be jubilant with joy! Sing to God, sing praises to his name; lift up a song to him who rides through the deserts; his name is the Lord; exult before him! Father of the fatherless and protector of widows is God in his holy habitation."**

- Ecclesiastes 9:5-6 - **"For the living know that they will die, but the dead know nothing, and they have no more reward, for the memory of them is forgotten. Their love and their hate and their envy have already perished, and forever they have no more share in all that is done under the sun."**

- Ecclesiastes 9:10 - **"Whatever your hand finds to do, do it with your might, for there is no work or thought or knowledge or wisdom in Sheol, to which you are going."**

- 1 Kings 3:16-28 - **"Then two prostitutes came to the king and stood before him. The one woman said, "Oh, my lord, this woman and I live in the same house, and I gave birth to a child while she was in the house. Then on the third day after I gave birth, this woman also gave birth. And we were alone. There was no one else** with us in the house; only we two were in the house. And this woman's son died in the night, because she lay on him. And she arose at midnight and took my son from beside me, while your servant slept, and laid him at her breast, and laid her dead son at my breast."

- Matthew 18:18 - **"Truly, I say to you, whatever you bind on earth shall be bound in heaven, and whatever you loose on earth shall be loosed in heaven."**

- Luke 16:19-31 - **"There was a rich man who was clothed in purple and fine linen and who feasted sumptuously every day. And at his gate was laid a poor man named Lazarus, covered with sores, who desired to be fed with what fell from the rich man's table. Moreover, even the dogs came and licked his sores. The poor man died and was carried by the angels to Abraham's side. The rich man also died and was buried, and in Hades, being in torment, he lifted up his eyes and saw Abraham far off and Lazarus at his side."**

- 1 John 4:1 **Beloved, do not believe every spirit, but test the spirits to see whether they are from God, for many false prophets have gone out into the world."**

- 1 Timothy 4:1 - **"Now the Spirit expressly says that in later times some will depart from the faith by devoting themselves to deceitful spirits and teachings of demons,"**

- 2 Corinthians 11:14-15 - **And no wonder, for even Satan disguises himself as an angel of light. So it is no surprise if his servants, also, disguise themselves as servants of righteousness. Their end will correspond to their deeds."**

- Job 7:9-10 - **"As the cloud fades and vanishes, so he who goes down to Sheol does not come up; he returns no more to his house, nor does his place know him anymore."**

- Galatians 5:20 - **"Idolatry, sorcery, enmity, strife, jealousy, fits of anger, rivalries, dissensions, divisions,"**

- Revelation 21:8 - **"But as for the cowardly, the faithless, the detestable, as for murderers, the sexually immoral, sorcerers, idolaters, and all liars, their portion will be in the lake that burns with fire and sulfur, which is the second death."**

- Revelation 22:15 - **"Outside are the dogs and sorcerers and the sexually immoral and murderers and idolaters, and everyone who loves and practices falsehood."**

- Revelation 18:23 - **"And the light of a lamp will shine in you no more, and the voice of bridegroom and bride will be heard in you no more, for your merchants were the great ones of the earth, and all nations were deceived by your sorcery."**

4.4 WHAT A PROPHETIC LESSON SHOULD ENTAIL

4.4.1 ☐ A[37] prophetic lesson will always match the words from God.

4.4.2 ☐ Prophetic lessons remind the church of God's promises.

4.4.3 ☐ Prophetic lessons always use prophetic language and symbolism.

4.4.4 ☐ Prophetic lessons explain God's methods and will.

4.4.5 ☐ Prophetic lessons help explain waiting.

4.4.6 ☐ Prophetic lessons encourage the church to pray before taking actions.

4.4.7 ☐ Prophetic lessons help order the churches steps into God's will.

4.4.8 ☐ Prophetic lessons remind the church that God rewards faith.

4.4.9 ☐ Prophetic lessons help explain God's silence.

4.4.10 ☐ Prophets can see into people's heart and prophetic lessons help heal hearts, and open hearts to the Holy Spirit.

4.4.11 ☐ Prophetic lessons remind the church to follow God's plan.

4.4.12 ☐ Prophetic lesson remind church that prayer tests prophecy and confirms its completion.

4.4.13 ☐ Prophetic lessons make God's instructions clear.
4.4.14 ☐ Prophetic lessons help faith grow.
4.4.15 ☐ Prophetic lessons help interpret dreams and visions.
4.4.16 ☐ Prophetic lessons remind the church that God is still in charge but does not always inform us of His plans.
4.4.17 ☐ Prophetic lessons help the church flow through challenging times and builds hope.
4.4.18 ☐ Prophetic lessons remind the church that God uses other people to fulfil His word.
4.4.19 ☐ Prophetic lessons remind the church that God speaks with precision, and we need to listen to God's words carefully, and do not change what He said.
4.4.20 ☐ Prophetic lessons teach us how to learn God's voice.
4.4.21 ☐ Prophetic lessons teach us to recognize God moving.
4.4.22 ☐ Prophetic lessons remind the church that God speaks in unexpected ways.
4.4.23 ☐ Scripture clarity - What is the main point of my text? - An effective sermon should ensure your text supports the truth, not your sermon.
4.4.24 ☐ Sermon clarity - What is the main point of my sermon? Ensure that your sermon is based

on and reinforces the truth, not opinion.

4.4.25 ☐ Sermon purpose - What is the motivation behind the sermon? All sermons should conform to the Triune Learning System® which is all about God.

    4.4.25.1 The Lesson - What we see in Christ and what we should emulate

    4.4.25.2 The Teacher - What we are told by Christ and what we should teacher others

    4.4.25.3 The Student - What we learn from Christ and or how to apply His words to our lives

4.4.26 ☐ What is at stake? - What if the truths of this passage are not obeyed? Use of the prophetic warnings and Gods judgements against the church.

4.4.27 ☐ Supporting documentation for the sermon? - Use simple clear, gripping illustrations and support to make the lesson both understandable and memorable.

4.4.28 ☐ What stories, examples, illustrations, and creative elements will help people see, feel and respond to the sermon? Use texts and parables which illustrate application of the sermon contents.

4.4.29 ☐ How should the sermon end? Does not always have to end with invitation make the sermon responsive to the Spirit and be flexible.

4.4.30 ☐ Do I need to make the sermon shorter? - 35 minutes is a long speech, try not to go long or break it up with illustrations and stories.

4.4.31 ☐ Does my life embody this message? - Bring God to life via the sermon.

4.4.32 ☐ Is there an equal emphasis on the word and the Spirit? - During the sermon, people should encounter God's Word and God's Spirit. Bring the entire experience to life.

4.4.33 ☐ Is this sermon rooted in love? - I want people to feel God's love and be drawn to Him through the sermon.

4.4.34 ☐ Will I trust the outcome to God? - God will make the difference; the sermon should invite God into the church and our lives. We just deliver the sermon; God delivers the souls.

4.5
WHAT MAKES AN EFFECTIVE PROPHET?

"Before I formed thee in the belly I knew thee; and before thou camest forth out of the womb I sanctified thee, and I ordained thee a prophet unto the nations. Be not afraid of their faces: for I am with thee to deliver thee, saith the LORD. Then the LORD put forth his hand and touched my mouth. And the LORD said unto me, Behold, I have put my words in thy mouth. See, I have this day set thee over the nations and over the kingdoms, to root out, and to pull down, and to destroy, and to throw down, to build, and to plant." - (Jeremiah 1:5, 8, 9, 11)

The Prophet has a unique calling. Unlike the other offices, the Prophet is called to serve in truth and obedience, there is no room in the prophetic for opinion and personal input. Please take time to look at list and tick of which elements you lack and how you plan to upgrade your arsenal.

4.5.1 **Wisdom**
- [ ] Knowledge
- [ ] Competency
- [ ] Fluency of topic and related topics
- [ ] Honesty

4.5.2 **Knowledge**
- [ ] Knowledge of teaching
- [ ] The characteristics of knowledge
- [ ] Interesting
- [ ] Informative
- [ ] Truthful
- [ ] Ever training

4.5.3 **Pondering proverbs**
- [ ] Considering existing wisdom
- [ ] Understanding existing wisdom

4.5.4 **Arranging proverbs**
- [ ] Conforming to existing wisdom
- [ ] Interpolating new

4.5.5 Use of acceptable words
- ☐ Not using profanity
- ☐ Not intimidating
- ☐ Truthful
- ☐ Not politically correct

4.5.6 Inoffensive
- ☐ Not opinionated
- ☐ Know when and where to use provocative words
- ☐ Relate words of truth
- ☐ Uncompromising

4.5.7 Words of truth
- ☐ Always teach the truth and not opinion
- ☐ If you only have opinion and rhetoric it is not teaching, it is conditioning

4.5.8 Simple
- ☐ LCS-Lowest common scripture
- ☐ Teach to the lowest level of the scripture without changing the meaning for cake of clarity
- ☐ Teach at a speed so that no one is confused
- ☐ Teach so that no one is left behind

4.5.9 Increasing knowledge
- ☐ Must increase the level of knowledge
- ☐ Must modify the level of understanding
- ☐ Must increase awareness
- ☐ Must increase influence of the Holy Spirit

4.5.11 Bring student closer to the God
- ☐ The Holy Spirit convicts
- ☐ A lesson that tries to sway or persuade is argumentative not informative
- ☐ A Prophet's job is to remind the church of God's will, despite the times
- ☐ This is the difference between education and revelation, revelation is exposure to God

4.6
MODULAR QUESTIONS FOR PROPHETIC CANDIDATE[38]

"Follow after charity, and desire spiritual gifts, but rather that ye may prophesy. For he that speaketh in an unknown tongue speaketh not unto men, but unto God: for no man understandeth him; howbeit in the spirit he speaketh mysteries. But he that prophesieth speaketh unto men to edification, and exhortation, and comfort. He that speaketh in an unknown tongue edifieth himself; but he that prophesieth edifieth the church. I would that ye all spake with tongues but rather that ye prophesied: for greater is he that prophesieth than he that speaketh with tongues, except he interprets, that the church may receive edifying. Now, brethren, if I come unto you speaking with tongues, what shall I profit you, except I shall speak to you either by revelation, or by knowledge, or by prophesying, or by doctrine? And even things without life giving sound, whether pipe or harp, except they give a distinction in the sounds, how shall it be known what is piped or harped? For if the trumpet give an uncertain sound, who shall prepare himself to the battle? So likewise, ye, except ye utter by the tongue words easy to be understood, how shall it be known what is spoken? for ye shall speak into the air. There are, it may be, so many kinds of voices in the world, and none of them is without signification. Therefore, if I know not the meaning of the voice, I shall be unto him that speaketh a barbarian, and he that speaketh shall be a barbarian unto me. Even so ye, forasmuch as ye are zealous of spiritual gifts, seek that ye may excel to the edifying of the church. Wherefore let him that speaketh in an unknown tongue pray that he may interpret. For if I pray in an unknown tongue, my spirit prayeth, but my understanding is unfruitful. What is it then? I will pray with the spirit, and I will pray with the understanding also: I will sing with the spirit, and

I will sing with the understanding also. Else when thou shalt bless with the spirit, how shall he that occupieth the room of the unlearned say Amen at thy giving of thanks, seeing he understandeth not what thou sayest? For thou verily givest thanks well, but the other is not edified. I thank my God, I speak with tongues more than ye all: Yet in the church I had rather speak five words with my understanding, that by my voice I might teach others also, than ten thousand words in an unknown tongue. Brethren, be not children in understanding: howbeit in malice be ye children, but in understanding be men. In the law it is written, With men of other tongues and other lips will I speak unto this people; and yet for all that will they not hear me, saith the Lord. Wherefore tongues are for a sign, not to them that believe, but to them that believe not: but prophesying serveth not for them that believe not, but for them which believe. If therefore the whole church be come together into one place, and all speak with tongues, and there come in those that are unlearned, or unbelievers, will they not say that ye are mad? But if all prophesy, and there come in one that believeth not, or one unlearned, he is convinced of all, he is judged of all: And thus, are the secrets of his heart made manifest; and so falling down on his face he will worship God, and report that God is in you of a truth. How is it then, brethren? when ye come together, every one of you hath a psalm, hath a doctrine, hath a tongue, hath a revelation, hath an interpretation. Let all things be done unto edifying. If any man speaks in an unknown tongue, let it be by two, or at the most by three, and that by course; and let one interpret. But if there be no interpreter, let him keep silence in the church; and let him speak to himself, and to God. Let the prophets speak two or three, and let the other judge. If anything, be revealed to another that sitteth by, let the first hold his peace. For ye may all prophesy one by one, that all may learn, and all may be comforted. And the spirits of the prophets are subject to the prophets. For God is not the author of confusion, but of peace, as in all churches of the saints. Let your women keep silence in the churches: for it is not permitted unto them to speak; but they are commanded to be under obedience as also saith the

> **law. And if they will learn anything, let them ask their husbands at home: for it is a shame for women to speak in the church. What? came the word of God out from you? or came it unto you only? If any man think himself to be a prophet, or spiritual, let him acknowledge that the things that I write unto you are the commandments of the Lord. But if any man be ignorant, let him be ignorant. Wherefore, brethren, covet to prophesy, and forbid not to speak with tongues. Let all things be done decently and in order**." - (1 Corinthians 14).

Ask these questions in conjunction with primary vocation as most persons claiming these titles are already ecumenically employed as a laity person of pastor. In my opinion, Apostles, Evangelists and Prophets should be able to answer all the questions of the Elders, deacons, and pastors as well as their particular calling, as their calling sits in a higher level of either responsibility or authority.

Paul felt it important enough to elucidate all this information about Prophets, Prophecy, and the responsibilities and responsive that should be present in same. These questions compromise the list, the Apostolic or Prophetic candidate, in addition to their basic duties and areas of knowledge should be able to answer all the questions included on lists 3.2-3.6. These (in my opinion) are the most abused and dangerous 'callings'. For these are the most difficult for the laity to challenge and verify. Anyone saying they feel *called*, should be watched carefully and followed only as the Word of God provides. I believe the Deacons and Elders are most needed when dealing with these callings, "...He placed the cherubim and a flaming sword that turned every way to guard the way to the Tree of Life."

_____
_____
_____
_____
_____
_____

4.6.1 Do you believe sin as the first step of restoration and should work to complete the process? Explain.
4.6.2 Can you discern sense when someone or something is not what it appears to be? Explain how, cite example of when.
4.6.3 How do you react to any form of clerical, or Christian deception or dishonesty?
4.6.4 Do you desire justice?

4.6.5 How do you provide a balance of truth and love?
4.6.6 Are you open about personal faults to dissuade legalism from themselves?
4.6.7 Which are you more loyal to truth and the mission than people?
4.6.8 Do you feel obliged to speak out against wrong?
4.6.9 Who should interpret prophecy?
4.6.10 Who should not interpret?
4.6.11 What is the main purpose of prophecy?
4.6.12 When or how should prophecy be given?
4.6.13 Can a prophet be wrong?
4.6.14 Can a prophecy be wrong?
4.6.15 Can a prophet decipher scriptural revelation?

5.0 Becoming a More Effective Evangelist

"But watch thou in all things, endure afflictions, do the work of an evangelist, make full proof of thy ministry," - (2 Timothy 4:5).

5.0
A DEFINITION OF EVANGELIST

Our definition of a. Evangelist is 'dispenser of good tidings' a missional-preacher of the gospel. This title applies to people who to go from place preaching the word. Evangelists often do not function in the authority of an apostle, nor the gift of prophecy, nor the responsibility of pastoral supervision. They were traveling preachers, having it as their special function to carry the gospel to places where it was previously unknown[39]."

5.1 TYPICAL EVANGELICAL DUTIES

- ☐ Oversee the regular and organized visitation of the church through planning, organizing and evaluating

- ☐ Develop church members to be personal witnesses of their Faith in Jesus

- ☐ Serve on the Missions Committee of the church as an exofficio member

- ☐ Serve on the Sunday School Council and other councils to give input as to evangelism

- ☐ Preach in the absence of the pastorate or when required by the church

- ☐ Assist the pastorate, staff and church in outreach and other community ministries

- ☐ Keep informed on evangelistic and witnessing resources, materials, methods, and administration; cooperating with denominational personnel, developments and interests

- ☐ Recommend an annual estimated budget for evangelistic and outreach needs

5.2 WHAT AN EVANGELISTIC LESSON SHOULD ENTAIL

Evangelistic lessons must also hold the basics. According to the church tradition, Evangelistic Lessons fall into one of #6 different evangelism styles. All six styles have hybrid delivery systems, but are consistent in terms of the message from God;

1. Apologetic / Intellectual
2. Confrontational
3. Testimonial
4. Interpersonal
5. Invitational
6. Service

5.2.1 ☐ Scripture Clarity - What is the main point of my text? An effective sermon should ensure your text supports the truth, not your sermon.

5.2.2 ☐ Sermon Clarity - What is the main point of my sermon? Ensure that your sermon is based on and reinforces the truth, not opinion.

5.2.3 ☐ Sermon Purpose - what is the motivation behind the sermon? All sermons should conform to the Triune Learning System® which is all about God.
    5.2.3.1 *The Lesson* - What we see in Christ and what we should emulate
    5.3.3.1 *The Teacher* - What we are told by Christ and what we should teacher others
    5.3.3.2 *The Student* - what we learn from Christ and or how to apply His words to our lives

5.2.4 ☐ What is at stake? What if the truths of this passage are not obeyed? Use of the prophetic warnings and God's judgements against the church

5.2.4 ☐ Supporting documentation for the sermon? Use simple clear, gripping illustrations and support to make the lesson both understandable and memorable.

5.2.5 ☐ What stories, examples, illustrations, and creative elements will help people see, feel, and respond to the sermon? - Use texts and parables which illustrate application of the sermon contents.

5.2.6 ☐ How should the sermon end? - Does not always have to end with invitation, make the sermon responsive to the spirit and be flexible.

5.2.7 ☐ Can I make the sermon shorter? - 35 minutes is a long speech, try not to go long, or break it up with illustrations and stories.

5.2.8 ☐ Lifestyle messages? - Bring God to life via the sermon.

5.2.9 ☐ Is there an equal emphasis on the word and the spirit? - During the sermon, people should encounter God's word and God's spirit. Bring the entire experience to life.

5.2.10 ☐ Is this sermon rooted in love? - I want people to feel God's love and be drawn to him through the sermon.

5.2.11 ☐ Will I trust the outcome to God? - God will make the difference; the sermon should invite God into the church and our lives. We just deliver the sermon; God delivers the souls.

_____
_____
_____
_____

5.3 WHAT MAKES AN EFFECTIVE EVANGELIST

Wisdom
- [ ] Knowledge
- [ ] Competency
- [ ] Fluency of topic and related topics
- [ ] Humility
- [ ] Compassion

Teaching knowledge
- [ ] Knowledge of teaching
- [ ] The characteristics of knowledge
- [ ] Interesting
- [ ] Informative
- [ ] Conforming to existing wisdom
- [ ] Truthful
- [ ] Ever training
- [ ] Amiable
- [ ] Understanding existing wisdom
- [ ] Interpolating new wisdom

Use of acceptable words
- [ ] Not using profanity
- [ ] Not intimidating
- [ ] Truthful
- [ ] Not politically correct

Inoffensive
- [ ] Not opinionated
- [ ] Know when and where to use provocative words
- [ ] Relate words of truth
- [ ] Learn colloquialisms and new terms used by younger people

Words of truth
- [ ] Always teach the truth and not opinion
- [ ] If you only have opinion and rhetoric it is not teaching, it is conditioning

Simple
- [ ] LCS…Lowest common student
- [ ] Teach to the lowest level of the audience

☐ Teach at a speed so that no one is confused

☐ Teach so that no one is left behind

Increasing knowledge
☐ Must increase the level of knowledge
☐ Must modify the level of understanding

☐ Must increase awareness
☐ Must increase student horizons and scope of thought

Bring student closer to the truth
☐ The truth convicts
☐ A lesson that tries to sway or persuade is argumentative not informative

☐ This is the difference between intelligence and education
☐ Education is more akin to indoctrination - teaching is more like exposure

Release the students mind to grow
☐ Free the student minds to grow

☐ Teach them how to formulate a thought

Use as a building block
☐ Learn how to think
☐ Learn how to build on these blocks

☐ Wisdom comes from above

_____
_____
_____
_____
_____
_____
_____
_____

5.4 TOOLS NECESSARY FOR EVANGELISTS

5.4.1 Prayer
- ☐ Maintains sensitivity to Holy Spirit
- ☐ Helps keep God involved

5.4.2 Your personal testimony
- ☐ Keeps both parties grounded
- ☐ Develops personal relationship and trust

5.4.3 Current stories of God's activity in your life
- ☐ Helps bring testimony to life
- ☐ Helps keep the attention

5.4.4 A version of the gospel in a nutshell[40]
- ☐ The simpler the better
- ☐ Simple but accurate, do not make understating more important than imparting the truth.

5.4.5 Poling
- ☐ Always poll the audience with questions, or by opening the floor with questions.
- ☐ This allows for more feedback and gets them involved.

5.4.6 Anime
- ☐ Despite what type style you use anime is necessary
- ☐ Can be the use of color
- ☐ Can be the use of jokes
- ☐ Can be the use of voice inflection
- ☐ Can be the use or movement

5.4.7 Pliability

- ☐ You must be able to answer questions handle criticism or Explain supporting concepts

5.5 EVANGELICAL CANDIDATE QUESTIONS[41]

Without a basic fluence in these areas, the candidate will be of no use to the kingdom and invariably end up lost and off track availing themselves nothing and the flock, a serving of platitudes, not revelation. These questions compromise a list of basic areas requiring coverage from every Evangelical candidate, as they cover the basic duties and areas of knowledge.

5.5.1   What is there about this position that excites and interests you?

5.5.2   What are your strongest abilities, experience and skills that will enable you to be effective in this position?

5.5.3   What are the major qualities you look for in your relationships with members of the congregation and/or your peers on the staff?

5.5.4   How do you prefer to work with others to achieve your objective?

5.5.5   Tell us about yourself: health, maturity and practical judgment, sense of humor, initiative.

5.5.6   We are interested in your leadership capabilities:

5.5.7   Describe your effectiveness as a preacher

5.5.8   Describe your effectiveness in evangelism

5.5.9 Describe your program effectiveness
5.5.10 Describe your Administrative ability
5.5.11 Describe your style of working with others
5.5.12 What large hopes and dreams have you for this congregation?
5.5.13 Tell us about your past relationship with earlier presbyteries.
5.5.14 What 'motivates' you and 'keeps you going'?
5.5.15 What areas of your ministry have been most exciting to you?
5.5.16 What is your understanding of faith?
5.5.17 Where are you in your pilgrimage of faith?
5.5.18 Tell us about your faith in Jesus Christ and personal religious life
5.5.19 What issues of theological reflection have been demanding your study and thinking recently?
5.5.20 Where are you at the present time in your theological studies?
5.5.21 What in your opinion is the foremost theological issue facing the Church today?
5.5.22 Explain Salvation
5.5.23 Explain faith
5.5.24 Explain grace

5.5.25 Stewardship of all of life How do you understand our role as stewards?

5.5.26 Describe your practice of Baptism

5.5.27 What do you see as the mission of the Church in the world?

5.5.28 Talk about your understanding of the church and its relationship with society

6.0 Becoming a More Effective Deacon

"In the same way, deacons are to be worthy of respect, sincere, not indulging in much wine, and not pursuing dishonest gain. They must keep hold of the deep truths of the faith with a clear conscience. They must first be tested; and then if there is nothing against them, let them serve as deacons'" - (1 Timothy 3:8-11).

6.0
A DEFINITION OF DEACON

Our definition of a Deacon derives from the Greek word *diákonos*, which is a standard ancient Greek word meaning 'servant', 'waiting-man', "minister", or 'messenger[42]'. Deacons have an important biblical role of taking care of the physical and logistical needs of the church. Deacons should expect to teach as the need arises whether as primary or to fill vacancies.

6.1 TYPICAL DEACON RESPONSIBILITIES AND DUTIES

- ☐ Participate regularly in a church group, either as a worker or a member
- ☐ Attend worship services and night activities, unless providentially hindered
- ☐ Actively serve in some ministry in the life of the church
- ☐ Be supportive of the overall ministry of the church
- ☐ Participate in all scheduled deacon activities, unless providentially hindered
- ☐ Be available to minister when called upon by Pastorate
- ☐ Practice personal evangelism of the lost as opportunities arise
- ☐ Attend beneficial training sessions as available, unless providentially hindered
- ☐ Pray for and support of the Pastorate, all staff, and deacon body

_____
_____
_____
_____
_____
_____
_____

6.2
WHAT DEACONS SHOULD TEACH

6.2.1 Prayer[43] - Without prayer the Christian walk is impossible.
6.2.2 The Necessity for Change - Without this the Christian walk is impossible.
6.2.3 Understating Trials - Deacons should emphasis that trials are not punitive they are a maturing method.
6.2.4 Servanthood - Silently and humbly serving in the position.
6.2.5 Pastors are accountable to God
6.2.6 Church - Belongs to God deacons serve for Him and they are accountable to Him.
6.2.7 Unity - As members jointly fitted together the church thrives and flourishes.
6.2.8 Submission - Is integral to unity.
6.2.9 Fellowship - Is a primary function of church and deacons need to aid this function whether physically of as facilitators.
6.2.10 Courage - We must be willing and able to defend the faith, in the face of sacrifice and persecution.
6.2.11 Sobriety - The church must remain sober and guarded against the enemy and to protect those entrusted to us.

_____
_____
_____
_____
_____
_____
_____
_____

6.3
WHAT MAKES AN EFFECTIVE DEACON

Wisdom
- [ ] Knowledge
- [ ] Competency

Teaching knowledge
- [ ] Knowledge of teaching
- [ ] Interesting
- [ ] Informative
- [ ] Conforming to existing wisdom
- [ ] Truthful
- [ ] Ever training

Use of acceptable words
- [ ] Not using profanity
- [ ] Not intimidating
- [ ] Truthful
- [ ] Not politically correct

Inoffensive
- [ ] Not opinionated
- [ ] Relate words of truth

Words of truth
- [ ] Always teach the truth and not opinion

Simple
- [ ] Teach to the lowest level of the congregation
- [ ] Teach at a speed so that no one is confused

Increasing knowledge
- [ ] Must change the level of understanding
- [ ] Must increase awareness
- [ ] Must increase student horizons and scope of thought

6.4
NECESSARY DEACON TOOLS

Deacons are a staple in God's organization. One of the two required officers to have a church. All other ministries are for perfecting the saints; the deacon and elder are for the protection of the saints. Like any other servant deacons need tools as well[44].

6.4.1 Spiritual mindedness - Allows deacons to abide by and pass on the words of Christ.

6.4.2 Effective workers - Deacons must be willing and able to do menial tasks needed to keep the church on order.

6.4.3 Submit to leadership - Humility and submission to leadership reduces friction and makes the mission move more effectively.

6.4.4 Maturation - Deacons must study and train often, to support their efficacy.

6.4.5 Level headedness - Growth and stability need change and as needed

6.4.6 - Studying the Bible

6.5.7 - Reliance on God

6.5 QUESTIONS FOR THE DEACON CANDIDATE

These questions compromise a list of basic areas requiring coverage from every Deacon candidate, as they cover the basic duties and areas of knowledge. Without a basic fluence in these areas, the candidate will be of no use to the kingdom and invariably end up serving the pastor, not God.

6.5.1 Explain your concept of God.
6.5.2 What is the Trinity?
6.5.3 Do Christians worship one God-or three?
6.5.4 Explain your understanding of God's grace.
6.5.5 How would you explain to an unbeliever how he or she may experience God's salvation?
6.5.6 What do you believe about the Bible?
6.5.7 What is the Bible's inspiration?
6.5.8 What is the Bible's authority?
6.5.9 What is the Bible's usefulness in today's world?
6.5.10 What is the Bible's its place in your own life?
6.5.11 Explain Christian stewardship?
6.5.12 What are the ordinances of the church?
6.5.13 What do you believe about the creation of mankind?

6.5.14 What role does prayer play in your life?

6.5.15 Why was Jesus Christ born and why did he die?

6.5.16 What do the Scriptures say about Jesus Christ's second coming?

6.5.17 What is the ministry of the Holy Spirit?

6.5.18 What is the baptism of the Holy Spirit?

6.5.19 What are the duties of a deacon?

6.5.20 What are some ways that a deacon is to be an example to others, both in and out of the church?

6.5.21 Is your wife supportive of your service?

6.5.22 Is your home life consistent with the teachings of Scripture?

6.5.23 What is the Bible's stance on marriage, divorce, remarriage?

6.5.24 What is the Bible's stance on race and racism, sexual purity (including chastity, cohabitation, living together sexually without marriage, promiscuity, and homosexuality)?

6.5.25 Please share how you came to know and follow Jesus Christ.

6.5.26 How long have you been a believer?

6.5.27 How long have you been a member of this church?

6.5.28 What are some of the ways you have served Jesus Christ through the church?

6.5.29 What does it mean to you that a deacon is to be 'filled with the Spirit?' Comment on the importance of the fruit of the Spirit in the life of a Christian leader.

6.5.30 How can deacons reflect the love of Christ?

7.0 Becoming a More Effective Elder / Bishop / Overseer

"To the elders among you, I appeal as a fellow elder and a witness of Christ's sufferings who also will share in the glory to be revealed: Be shepherds of God's flock that is under your care, watching over them-not because you must, but because you are willing, as God wants you to be; not pursuing dishonest gain, but eager to serve; not lording it over those entrusted to you, but being examples to the flock. And when the Chief Shepherd appears, you will receive the crown of glory that will never fade away." - (1 Peter 5:1-9).

7.0
A DEFINITION OF ELDER

Our definition of an Elder is an elder is an ordained person who usually serves a local church or churches, ordained to a ministry of word, sacrament, and order, filling the preaching and pastoral offices[45].

The primary spiritual leaders of a congregation are the elders, referred to as bishops or overseers in the New Testament. Unlike deacons, Elders focus less on physical stewardship and more on spiritual stewardship.

Despite Ecumenical convention the Elders have set duties that are unique to them. Before we cover them, and elder may have added duties and occupy another ministry position such as pastor etc, but the job requirements of the elder do not deviate. I believe that meshing the duties does not alter the biblical edicts and if we mesh then the elder duty must override the other. For example, of an elder is the presiding pastor that is fine, but when it comes to discipline the pastor should not be involved, they should resign themselves to allow the active elders to do their jobs. Elders help keep discipline, pray for the sick and interpret prophecy and tongues (James 5:14-16, 1 Timothy 3:1-16, 1 Timothy 5:17-18). According to the Bible these tasks is assigned to the office, not the man.

7.1 TYPICAL ELDER RESPONSIBILITIES AND DUTIES

- ☐ Elders must be members of the church. Elders must be active in the life of the congregation's and give evidence of seeking to grow in their own understanding and practice of the Christian life. Such evidence should include, but not be limited to, the following:
- ☐ Conduct of one's life in light of the teachings of Jesus Christ.
- ☐ Promotion of good will and Christian fellowship in the congregation and community.
- ☐ Regular attendance at worship services and stated meetings of the congregation.
- ☐ Regular and faithful contributions to the support of the congregation and its outreach programs.
- ☐ Willingness to fulfill assignments on behalf of the congregation.

- ☐ Demonstrated gifts and skills or evident potential in carrying out the responsibilities of an elder.
- ☐ Share in the pastoral, church grow and teaching functions of the ministry
- ☐ Providing communion to the homebound.
- ☐ Serving as the shepherd for an assigned group of congregation members and regular visitors.
- ☐ Regularly communicate with your assigned to discuss any other matters of importance to them.
- ☐ Provide spiritual comfort and support to members both at church functions and away from church if requested. Monitor attendance of the members of your flock and contact them to discuss any concerns if there is a change in their attendance pattern.
- ☐ Attends the regular monthly elder's meeting.
- ☐ Attends and/or conducts Christian education classes.
- ☐ Participates in scheduled elder workshops and/or retreats.
- ☐ Prepare and present the communion meditation and communion prayer and preside at the communion table as the representative of the congregation.
- ☐ Help and/or conduct the service in the absence of the Pastorate.
- ☐ Give counsel about spiritual life and development of the congregation.
- ☐ All duties of deacon and usher

_____
_____
_____
_____
_____
_____
_____
_____
_____

7.2
WHAT ELDERS SHOULD TEACH[46]

Elders have two distinct jobs the flock and the deacons. The safeguard the flock but also teach and groom deacons.

7.2.1 **Elders teach how to settle disputes in the church** - (Acts 15:1-2, NLT). Elders help keep stability and discipline. Their authority comes from both the office and their relationship with the flock.

7.2.2 **Elders should teach how to pray for the sick** - Although we would love to see our pastor where we are ailing, that may not be possible, as they are just one person. The elders who can be as many as desired, have far more diversity than the pastor and work for the same God. Furthermore, they are tasked with healing, not the pastors (James 5:4).

7.2.3 **Elders should teach how to watch over and serve the church with humility** (1 Peter 5:1-4) - We oversee because we care not because we can. The can should come from love for God's sheep. Remember ae we oversee the flock that God feels for His sheep as David felt about the man who killed the one sheep. He has love for each and does not tolerate their abuse.

7.2.4 **Elders should teach how to watch over each other for the spiritual health of the flock** (Hebrews 13:17) - If elders can be instrumental in healing of the flesh, surly their relationship with God affords them spiritual discernment. There is no reason for elders to wait on the pastor to address or recognize when the flock is ill or hurting.

7.2.5 **Elders should teach the flock how to spend time in prayer and teaching the word** - We cannot hear from and teach God's words if we do not know them. Both the elder and the pastor are out of God's will and word when they allow deficient people to Eld. Usher and greeter is a nonspiritual position, but the two offices MUST BE SPIRITUAL MINDED AND IN PRACTICE.

7.3
WHAT MAKES AN EFFECTIVE ELDER

Wisdom
- [ ] Knowledge
- [ ] Competency
- [ ] Fluency of topic and related topics

Teaching knowledge
- [ ] Knowledge of teaching
- [ ] The characteristics of knowledge
- [ ] Interesting
- [ ] Informative
- [ ] Truthful
- [ ] Ever training

Pondering proverbs
- [ ] Considering existing wisdom
- [ ] Understanding existing wisdom

Arranging proverbs
- [ ] Conforming to existing wisdom
- [ ] Interpolating new wisdom

Use of acceptable words
- [ ] Not using profanity
- [ ] Not intimidating
- [ ] Truthful
- [ ] Not politically correct

Inoffensive
- [ ] Not opinionated
- [ ] Know when and where to use provocative words
- [ ] Relate words of truth

Words of truth
- [ ] Always teach the truth and not opinion
- [ ] If you only have opinion and rhetoric it is not teaching, it is conditioning

Simple
- [ ] LCS…Lowest common student

- [ ] Teach to the lowest level of the audience
- [ ] Teach at a speed so that no one is confused
- [ ] Teach so that no one is left behind

Increasing knowledge
- [ ] Must increase the level of knowledge
- [ ] Must change the level of understanding
- [ ] Must increase awareness
- [ ] Must increase student horizons and scope of thought

Bring student closer to the truth
- [ ] The truth convicts
- [ ] A lesson that tries to sway or persuade is argumentative not informative
- [ ] This is the difference between intelligence and education
- [ ] Education is more akin to indoctrination - teaching is more like exposure

_____
_____
_____
_____
_____
_____
_____
_____
_____
_____
_____
_____
_____

7.4
NECESSARY ELDER TOOLS

Elders are a staple in God's organization, one of the two that are required. All other ministries are for the perfecting of the saints the deacon and elder are for the protection sf the saints. Like any other servant elders need tools as well[47].

7.4.1 Spiritual mindedness - Allows deacons to abide by and pass on the words of Christ.
7.4.2 Effective workers - Deacons must be willing and able to do menial tasks needed to keep the church on order.
7.4.3 Submit to leadership - Humility and submission to leadership reduces friction and makes the mission move more effectively.
7.4.4 Maturation - Deacons must study and train often, to keep their efficacy.
7.4.5 Level headedness - Growth and stability needs the ability to change and as needed
7.4.6 Bible study
7.4.7 Reliance on God
7.4.8 Self-control

7.5
QUESTIONS FOR ELDER CANDIDATES[48]

These questions compromise a list of basic areas requiring coverage from every Elder candidate, as they cover the basic duties and areas of knowledge. Without a basic fluence in these areas, the candidate will be of no use to the kingdom and invariably end up serving the pastor, not God.

7.5.1   Divorce and remarriage. Is there an allowable basis, and if so what is it?
7.5.2   Can a person who divorced be remarried?
7.5.3   What are the Gifts of the Holy Spirit?
7.5.4   Are all the Gifts of the Holy Spirit still being used?
7.5.5   What is the purpose/calling of an Elder?
7.5.6   What is the purpose of the Church?
7.5.7   How do I /can I know God's will? What is God's will for our lives?
7.5.8   Explain salvation
7.5.9   Is it okay for Christians to date a non-Christians?
7.5.10 What is the purpose of missions?
7.5.11 How do you know the bible is God's word…why is it different than other books that claim to be divine?
7.5.12 Do Christians need to obey the Old Testament Law?
7.5.13 What does it mean to be filled with the Spirit?
7.5.14 How do you live the spiritual life?
7.5.15 Aren't all religions the same? What makes Christianity different? What is your basic understanding of Muslim, Buddhism, Hinduism, Mormonism, Jehovah's Witness, New Age Movement, and Unitarianism?
7.5.16 Be able to discuss the philosophies of the day (post-modernism, fatalism, nihilism, naturalism, relativism, etc.)
7.5.17 Why do trials occur, and suffering happen?
7.5.18 What is purpose of James 5?
7.5.19 What is God's position on homosexuality?

7.5.20 Are people born this way?
7.5.21 How do you answer those who believe that redefining marriage to include same-gender couples (or any other redefinition of marriage)?
7.5.22 Why does doctrinal competency matter?
7.5.23 What is a seeker service?
7.5.24 Is it okay for believers to drink?
7.5.25 Is tithing biblical? What is different between Old and New Testament giving?
7.5.26 Is debt biblically allowable? Should Christians have debt? Are there diverse types of debt?
7.5.27 Should we ever recommend a licensed counselor?
7.5.28 What does it mean to counsel biblically?
7.5.29 What is community?
7.5.30 What is accountability?
7.5.31 Are there any areas that are off-limits within an accountability relationship?
7.5.32 Should we be a place that is "confidential" or "safe"? What is the difference
7.5.33 What is Baptism?
7.5.34 Is baptism necessary?
7.5.35 Differentiate between creation, evolution, and theories of Genesis 1.
7.5.36 Is it okay for believers to use contraception?

_____
_____
_____
_____
_____
_____
_____

8.0 BECOMING A MORE EFFECTIVE APOSTLE

"Truly the signs of an apostle were wrought among you in all patience, in signs, and wonders, and mighty deeds," - (Corinthians 3:3).

8.0
A DEFINITION OF APOSTLE

"For I speak to you Gentiles, inasmuch as I am the apostle of the Gentiles, I magnify mine office."
(Romans 11:13).

For our purposes lets define an Apostle as, an ambassador or special witness of the whose function is to teach the principles of salvation outside the walls of the church. But an Apostle according to the duties undertaken in the Bible, also holds high authority within the church to maintaining Kingdom integrity. Much like a governmental Ambassador, this person having spoken to the head, and conferring with the head relays the directives of the king or reminds of the directives of the king. As they speak for the King, they have the authority of the Kingdom at their back (no direct authority however) and carry with them the authority to speak into church misgivings and mis-management.

As an added responsibility of this office, more so than all the others (except the Prophet) there is no room for ego, and pride. The Ambassador represents the King, not the church; and therefore, must always do such with the utmost transparency and accountability.

8.1 BASIC QUALIFICATIONS OF AN APOSTLE

According to scripture (Mark 3:14-15) Apostles;

8.1.1 Must have a good relationship with the Holy Spirt - (Mark 3:14-15)

8.1.2 Must be completely obedient - (Mark 3:14-15)

8.1.3 Operate under the authority to do Christ's work - (Mark 3:14-15)

8.1.4 Submission to Christ - not a law unto themselves - (Philippians 2:5-8)

8.1.5 Willingness to suffer for Christ - (Colossians 1:24-29)

8.1.6 Holiness - (2 Corinthians 1:3)
8.1.7 Sincerity - (2 Corinthians 1:3)
8.1.8 Have grace on their lives - (2 Corinthians 1:3)

8.2
DEVELOPMENT OF THE APOSTOLIC CALLING

As this is function finds itself less prominent, I found an interesting article on this matter that gives as sound overview of duties and development of the Apostolic calling. I have synthesized the information and simplified it for this resource.

8.2.1 Most apostles do not start out as apostles. They start as preachers or teachers of the Word of God.

8.2.2 Everything they preach and teach is from the scriptures (I Timothy 2:7). They often seem borderline Legalistic[49].

8.2.3 Apostles train and equip disciple-makers (II Timothy 2:1-2).

8.2.4 The Apostles heart is to aid in the maturation of believers and their relationship with the Holy Spirit.

8.2.5 Apostles help activate, stir up, and release other people's gifts (II Timothy 1:6).

8.2.6 Apostles groom others to take their place and serve as they do, they do not fear competition.

8.2.7 An Apostle imparts what is lacking so the believer can rise to full maturity.

8.2.8 Apostles are spiritual mentors (II Timothy 4:14) that nurture and protect underlings.

8.2.9 An Apostle can help people grow into their full potentials

8.2.10 Apostles no longer write scripture. They build upon foundations laid. Remember, the Apostle works under authority they therefore must constantly assert and remind of the authority they represent.

8.2.11 Apostles have access to revelations and the unfolding of mysteries (Galatians 1:11-3).

8.2.12 Apostles bring Prophecy into practice and guidance within the church. Apostles bring order and government to the Church. Government is necessary to help the flow of God's power and anointing Titus 1:5.

8.2.13 An apostle who is sent to a city has spiritual authority in that city in the spirit over those demons therein. Apostles who flee and or fear ritual warfare is working outside their calling.

8.2.14 Sadly, Apostles decree judgment and correction to the Church. The prophecies set forth, are for all of God's people. Enacting their measure in certain places takes a little more refinement and more authority, as historically most believers do not heed prophets. Apostles are bishops, they oversee churches. Apostles ordain and set in place qualified leadership.

8.2.15 "The apostolic anointing is a confrontational anointing. Apostles confront false teaching, witchcraft, immorality and anything that will keep the church from fulfilling its purpose."

8.3
WHAT APOSTOLIC LESSONS SHOULD CONTAIN

    A lesson in this vein is s combination of the prophetic and the teacher. Jesus gives us the best example in …UPON THESE TWO, THE LAW HANGS. Here we have very technical teaching not intended for the unbeliever or the lay person. This lesson outlaid to the Scribes, Pharisees, and lawyers. The reason Jesus could condense the information into a synthesis of Old Testament Scripture was that He was correcting an application of scripture faulted by the church. He exerted His understanding and knowledge, to usurp the church elders' illegitimate authority, by showing them the errors in their understanding and application of the scripture.

    Jesus was 3 when He first responded to His apostolic calling. For this purpose, His teachings to the disciples were always cryptic in nature. We now call them kingdom keys, but they are still mysteries. As Jews, they knew most of the law, but their knowledge and application were flawed. Jesus spent most of His time with the 3 retraining them and debunking the church traditions and lies. In so doing He did two things. Firstly, deliver us from perpetual darkness. Secondly, He showed them how to and why to walk as Apostles; praying, casting out demons, and rebuking the false teacher.

    8.3.1 Apostolic lessons should always rely on the revelation of God's word, not rhetoric or barbarous applications of opinion. We can only convict or indict people on wat God does, never our opinion, need, greed or pride. Falsely accusing others is the devil's work; when we do this John 8:44 applies in full fervor. It was to this conviction the Pharisees wanted to kill Jesus, because He proved them to be accursed.

    8.3.2 Apostolic lessons should always correct immoral behavior or thinking, by using the straight edges provided by God. No apostle should speak and leave the church in the darkness, he then has not spoken under the authority of the Holy Spirit.

8.3.3 Apostolic lessons should be clear and definitive, and never waiver to the crowd. The Apostle sets and supports the standard. It is called a standard because it does not change.

8.3.4 Apostolic lessons should never pander to the laity or the host church. If they did not want to hear the truth they should not have invited, you. NO ONE walks into the king's hall (my father's house) and gives honor to the lesser person. No ambassador walks in and greets the servants, exulting them. It is God's house, honor Him in it. The people that serve in the house (pastor etc) should rejoice when you arrive and join you in the waiving of God's banner. No man sits Higher than God, therefore we should not exalt them as part of our lesson. Be gracious, not reverent.

8.3.5 Apostolic lessons must be crafter to teach all levels. But remember it not the apostle's job to bring the new, lost, confused into revelation. The apostle brings the teacher, pastors, deacon, elders and evangelists into revelation accordance, then the management style of reaching down and fishing them out of the filth ensues. Therefore, your lesson should inspire the outsiders, and educate and enlighten the insider.

8.4
WHAT APOSTOLIC LESSONS SHOULD NOT CONTAIN

No one wants to be reminded that they are inept. But this is what is exemplified by the Apostle make Himself. The problem with false teaching we articulated in the beginning of the book. We cannot afford for the sake of not stepping on toes, to listen to or allow false teaching to mislead or hold in bondage, any that the Father has given Him, or the lost.

8.4.1 Apostolic lessons should not have useless clichés and rhetoric. From and authority most things will be taken seriously, we cannot afford levity therefore. This does not mean no sense of humor, it just means be careful what you espoused as gospel.

8.4.2 Apostolic lesson should not contain politically correct language of information. This is not the same as tact. Crassness serves no one, but we must not change scripture because society has decided to modernize.

8.4.3 8.5.3 **Damnation should never be a part of the message.** There are hundreds of ways to warn against hell without judgmentally calling down the fire.

8.5
WHAT MAKES A MORE EFFECTIVE APOSTLE[50]

There is a difference between God's work and church work. There should not be this distinction, but it has always been there (Luke 4:5-9). What the church calls an apostle fails in comparison to Gods way. I complied additional materials on the apostleship[51].

Please take time to look at list and tick of which elements you lack and how you plan to upgrade your arsenal.

- 8.5.1 ☐ Biblical preaching
- 8.5.2 ☐ Preaching Christ
- 8.5.3 ☐ Preaching faith in Christ and repentance
- 8.5.4 ☐ Preaching the power of the Holy Spirit
- 8.5.5 ☐ Preach boldly
- 8.5.6 ☐ Empathy
- 8.5.7 ☐ Apostles of Christ build the Kingdom - According to the studies, 'church apostles' focus mainly on their local areas. The main reason given for this is they seem to be inclined to stay close to works areas they helped develop or minister to. However true apostles do not focus locally because God called them to the church universal. By going everywhere as commanded the apostles helps to engender unity in God's kingdom. This is no way means neglect those we see every day, but we need to keep planting seed.
- 8.5.8 ☐ Apostles of Christ are not Hierarchical - Church apostles often find themselves caught up in titles, and measures or affluence. Real apostles do not crave titles (they will use them only when needed, usually to thwart argumentative laity) and do not rely on church to validate their calling.
- 8.5.9 ☐ Apostles of Christ do not Strive for Recognition - Philippians 2 teaches us that Jesus made Himself of no reputation.
- 8.5.10 ☐ Apostles of Christ do not worship money - Apostles serve God, not material gain.

8.5.11 ☐ Apostles of Christ lay down their lives for the gospel - Obedience is better that sacrifice, apostles make sacrifices out of obedience to their call.

8.5.12 ☐ Apostles of Christ have a servant's heart - Apostles believe the message of Christ is far more important than the messenger of Christ.

8.5.13 ☐ Apostles of Christ have divine influence and calling beyond their network of churches - Apostles must enable themselves to be all things to mall men, all places. There is no comfort zone for the Apostle, except enlarging the Kingdom of their Master.

8.5.14 ☐ Apostles of Christ have an intimate walk with God - And strive to know God and to make Him known in their lives.

8.5.15 ☐ Apostles endure great hardship - Apostles endure discomfort and forgo most creature comforts for the love of their craft.

_____
_____
_____
_____
_____
_____
_____
_____
_____
_____
_____
_____
_____
_____
_____
_____
_____
_____
_____

Wisdom
- [ ] Knowledge
- [ ] Competency
- [ ] Fluency of topic and related topics

Knowledge
- [ ] Knowledge of teaching
- [ ] The characteristics of knowledge
- [ ] Interesting
- [ ] Informative
- [ ] Truthful
- [ ] Ever training

Pondering proverbs
- [ ] Considering existing wisdom
- [ ] Understanding existing wisdom

Arranging proverbs
- [ ] Conforming to existing wisdom
- [ ] Interpolating new wisdom

Use of acceptable words
- [ ] Not using profanity
- [ ] Not intimidating
- [ ] Truthful
- [ ] Not politically correct

Inoffensive
- [ ] Not opinionated
- [ ] Know when and where to use provocative words
- [ ] Relate words of truth

Words of truth
- [ ] Always teach the truth and not opinion
- [ ] If you only have opinion and rhetoric it is not teaching, it is conditioning

Simple
- [ ] LCS…Lowest common student
- [ ] Teach to the lowest level of the audience
- [ ] Teach at a speed so that no one is confused
- [ ] Teach so that no one is left behind

Increasing knowledge
- [ ] Must increase the level of knowledge
- [ ] Must modify the level of understanding
- [ ] Must increase awareness
- [ ] Must increase student horizons and scope of thought

Bring student closer to the truth
- [ ] The truth convicts
- [ ] A lesson that tries to sway or persuade is argumentative not informative
- [ ] An Apostle's job is to teach the church how to think not what to think
- [ ] This is the difference between intelligence and education
- [ ] Education is more akin to indoctrination - teaching is more like exposure

Release the church's mind to grow
- [ ] Teach them to make disciples
- [ ] Teach them how to formulate a thought

Use as a building block
- [ ] Learn how to think God's way
- [ ] Learn how to build on these blocks
- [ ] Wisdom comes from above

_____
_____
_____
_____
_____
_____
_____
_____
_____
_____
_____
_____

8.6 NECESSARY TOOLS FOR AN APOSTLE

8.6.1 Familial/spousal cooperation - Marriage is a work in and of itself, any intrusions or extra burdens often proves to be harmful or detrimental to a marriage. Therefore, a ministry partner MUST be supportive in at least assent and prayer else, the battle rages within the house itself.

8.6.2 Faith - The walk is hard, the fight brutal, carrying the war to the enemy a nightmare that cannot succeed without Hs joy and His strength (Matthew 9:29).

8.6.3 Ability to work within the ecumenical community foundations - This often means relationships which are rocky, dealing with bruised egos, contending with incompetence and corruption, as well as a healthy portion of insecurity and jealousy.

8.6.4 Resilience - "The dictionary definition of resilience is: the power or ability to return to the original form or position after being bent, compressed, or stretched; elasticity. The second definition is the ability to recover readily from illness, depression, adversity, or the like; buoyancy," sadly this too is part of the job. Learning how to deal with this is tremendously important to success of the person.

8.6.5 A great relationship with the Lord - The joy of the Lord must be our source or our strength and our joy, otherwise we fight in our own strength and posture. Usually creating Sinicism and dissolution.

8.6.6 High level of self-motivation - There is nothing to push except your love for God and your own passion, both are delicate and need constant monitoring and updating.

8.7
WARNINGS ABOUT FALSE APOSTLES

"Would to God ye could bear with me a little in my folly: and indeed bear with me. For I am jealous over you with godly jealousy: for I have espoused you to one husband, that I may present you as a chaste virgin to Christ. But I fear, lest by any means, as the serpent beguiled Eve through his subtilty, so your minds should be corrupted from the simplicity that is in Christ. For if he that cometh preacheth another Jesus, whom we have not preached, or if ye receive another spirit, which ye have not received, or another gospel, which ye have not accepted, ye might well bear with him. For I suppose I was not a whit behind the very chiefest apostles. But though I be rude in speech, yet not in knowledge; but we have been throughly made manifest among you in all things. Have I committed an offence in abasing myself that ye might be exalted, because I have preached to you the gospel of God freely? I robbed other churches, taking wages of them, to do you service. And when I was present with you, and wanted, I was chargeable to no man: for that which was lacking to me the brethren which came from Macedonia supplied: and in all things I have kept myself from being burdensome unto you, and so will I keep myself. As the truth of Christ is in me, no man shall stop me of this boasting in the regions of Achaia. Wherefore? because I love you not? God knoweth. But what I do, that I will do, that I may cut off occasion from them which desire occasion; that wherein they glory, they may be found even as we. For such are false apostles, deceitful workers, transforming themselves into the apostles of Christ. And no marvel; for Satan himself is transformed into an angel of light. Therefore, it is no great thing if his ministers also be transformed as the ministers of righteousness; whose end shall be according to their works. I say again, let no man think me a fool; if otherwise, yet as a fool receive me, that I may boast myself a little. That which I speak, I speak it not after the Lord, but as it were foolishly, in this confidence of boasting. Seeing that many glory after the flesh, I will glory also. For ye suffer fools gladly, seeing ye yourselves are wise. For ye suffer, if a man bring you into bondage, if a man devour you, if a man take of you, if a man exalt himself, if a man smite you on the face. I speak as concerning reproach, as though we had been weak. Howbeit wherein soever any is bold, (I speak foolishly,) I am bold also. Are they Hebrews? so am I. Are they Israelites? so am I. Are they the seed of Abraham? so am I. Are they ministers of Christ? (I speak as a fool) I am more; in labours more abundant, in stripes above measure, in prisons more frequent, in deaths oft. Of the Jews five times received I forty stripes save one. Thrice was I beaten with rods, once was I stoned, thrice I suffered shipwreck, a night and a day I have been in the deep; In journeyings often, in perils of waters, in perils of robbers, in perils by mine own countrymen, in perils by the heathen, in perils in the city, in perils in the wilderness, in perils in the sea, in perils among false brethren; In weariness and painfulness, in watchings often, in hunger and thirst, in fastings often, in cold and nakedness. Beside those things that are without, that which cometh upon me daily, the care of all the churches. Who is weak, and I am not weak? who is offended, and I burn not? If I must need glory, I will glory of the things which concern mine infirmities. The God and Father of our Lord Jesus Christ, which is blessed for evermore, knoweth that I lie not. In Damascus the governor under Aretas the king kept the city of the damascenes with a garrison, desirous to apprehend me: And through a window in a basket was I let down by the wall and escaped his hands**." (2 Corinthians 11).

As stated previously, in my opinion, Apostles, Evangelists and Prophets should be able to answer all the questions of the Elders, deacons and pastors as well as their particular calling, as their calling sits in a higher level of either responsibility or authority. Paul felt it important enough to elucidate all this information about Apostles, and the responsibilities and responsive that should be present in same.

Traits of the false apostle
    8.7.1 Boastful
        8.7.2 They lead believers astray from pure and sincere devotion to Christ
            (Gospel of Inclusion, unconditional acceptance, Gay is ok)
    8.7.3 They preach another Jesus and a different gospel ('Gospel of Inclusion,' 'unconditional acceptance,' 'Gay is ok')
    8.7.4 Always looking for validations
    8.7.5 Deceitful
    8.7.6 They push themselves forward, even to the point of abuse and control
    8.7.8 Quick to claim leadership
    8.7.9 Exclude others
    8.7.10 Grumblers
    8.7.11 Fault-finders
    8.7.12 Bold
    8.7.13 Arrogant
    8.7.14 Motivated by self-interest, greed
    8.7.15 Envious and insincere
    8.7.16 Despise authority

_____
_____
_____
_____
_____
_____
_____
_____
_____

8.8
MODULAR QUESTIONS FOR APOSTLE CANDIDATES

Ask these questions in conjunction with primary vocation as most persons claiming these titles are already ecumenically employed as a laity or pastor.

8.8.1 How are you set apart? _____

8.8.2 Are you a spiritual entrepreneur? _____

8.8.3 Tell about your call _____

8.8.4 When did you first acknowledge your calling? _____

8.8.5 What training and development have you under taken? _____

8.8.6 How do you deal with rejection and opposition? _____

8.8.7 Explain the call to forsake everything _____

8.8.8 Do you understand and please explain suffering for the call? _____

8.8.9 Explain the call to leadership _____

8.8.10 What is an Apostle? _____

8.8.11 What does and Apostle do?

8.8.12 Whose authority is an Apostle subject to?

8.8.13 Do you believe in al the gifts?

8.8.1 Do you have any gifts?

9.0 LEARNING THE STYLES OF AUDIENCE

"For though I am free from all *men,* I have made myself a servant to all, that I might win the more; and to the Jews I became as a Jew, that I might win Jews; to those *who are* under the law, as under the law, that I might win those *who are* under the law; to those *who are* without law, as without law (not being without law toward God, but under law toward Christ), that I might win those *who are* without law; to the weak I became as weak, that I might win the weak. I have become all things to all *men,* that I might by all means save some. Now this I do for the gospel's sake, that I may be partaker of it with you." (1 Corinthians 9:19-23).

9.1 LEARNING THE STYLES OF THE AUDIENCE[52]

Dynamic Style	Apologetic Style
Dialectical Style	Confrontational Style
Didactic Style	Testimonial Style
Demonstrative Style	Interpersonal Style
Animated Style	Invitational Style
Empirical Style	Service Style
Abstract Style	Linguistic Style
Argumentative Style	Naturalist Style
Command Style	Musical or Rhythmic Style
Practical Style	Learner Style
Reciprocal Style	Kinesthetic Style
Task Style	Visual or Spatial Style
Guided Discovery Style	Logical or Mathematical Style
Problem-Solving Style	Intrapersonal Style
Exploration Style	

The recipient of the information is the most important part of the lesson. Remember, they can be sheep without a shepherd, but the shepherd cannot exist without the sheep. It is for them we teach not to them. The study, preparation, and patience are all for them. If they do not learn from you, you are the problem.

Each hearer is different but fall into categories similar to styles determined for the teachers. Part of the teacher's job is to apply their knowledge of their skills against the personality of the student. The Chef's proficiency manifests itself in two manners; preparation and presentation of food. We prepare spiritual food and must use the same skill set.

    The lesson must be palatable to the student or they will not eat. If Jesus could look people in the eye and tell them they are going to hell successfully then there is no topic too difficult for us to handle.

9.2
LEARNING STYLES[53]

According to Dr. Rita Dunn[54], 'Learning style is the way in which each individual learner begins to concentrate on, process, absorb and retain new and difficult material.'

In article called, <u>Knowledge is power, Self-knowledge is powerful</u>, Dunn relates the following three important morsels of information about learning, students and teaching.

1. *Students* - When learners recognize their learning style with its various parameters there is an advantage to their learning protocols. They know how to absorb and absorb the material within the parameters of their style.

2. *Teachers* - Understanding that one learning sized does not fit all incorporate a variety of styles in their delivery system.

3. *Employers* - who appreciate diversity have an advantage over those who do not. They energies employees by liberating them from the one-size-fits-all mentality.

_____
_____
_____
_____
_____
_____
_____
_____
_____
_____

9.2.1
THE DYNAMIC LEARNING STYLE

- [ ] Is loud
- [ ] Is coarse
- [ ] Demands attention
- [ ] Is more interested in being seen than in learning

The way to deal with this type of student is to institute a recognition system such as raising hands or standing until you are asked to speak. The wait will annoy them and once they realize they cannot manipulate the class the will eventually listen.

9.2.2
THE DIALECTICAL LEARNING STYLE

☐ Loves to talk
☐ Asks many questions
☐ Debates and engages in questions

☐ Often tries to increase their awareness and knowledge by trying yours

The way to deal with this type of student is to answer their questions from an unforeseen angle and they also do not handle being incorrect well, walking through their error goes a long way in earning their trust. They can be helpful in terms of engaging the audience.

9.2.3
THE DIDACTIC LEARNING STYLE

☐ Is often urbane
☐ Is prone to humanistic causes

☐ Can only be swayed by knowledge, right and wrong is defined by their earlier studies of the human condition

The way to deal with this type of student is to use pure fact and reason to create a believer in them. Once they trust in your expertise, teaching them new things will be easy they will look up to you as a mentor. They will not be molded by moral persuasion.

9.2.4
THE DEMONSTRATIVE LEARNING STYLE

- [ ] More interested in method than results
- [ ] Simply likes to be seen, much like the dynamic
- [ ] Their kind of intellect is limited to what they can perceive with their senses
- [ ] Feels their way through every conflict

The way to deal with this type of student is to use examples and illustrations that evoke feelings. The method into their minds is to walk them through faulty decisions in their pasts that have caused pain and disillusion.

9.2.5
THE ANIMATED LEARNING STYLE

☐ Lives to theorize
☐ Enjoys stories and anecdotes
☐ Determines what they will accept as truth depending on whether they like the presenter

The way to deal with this type of student is to develop a report with the person. The objective teaching style does not work well with this personality they crave personal attention.

9.2.6
THE EMPIRICAL LEARNING STYLE

- ☐ Not interested in lively lessons and will often sit up front close to the teacher
- ☐ They will pout if the teacher is not filled with useful fact
- ☐ They will refer to notes and current affairs to ask questions
- ☐ They are very interested in learning the "why's" of any given topic

The way to deal with this type of student is to have a firm grasp of supporting topics. The teacher that has a proficiency in the topic and things related to it will develop an instant love affair with this student. They will even stay attached during disagreement if the contention is laudable.

9.2.7
THE ABSTRACT LEARNING STYLE

- [ ] Is often artsy
- [ ] Cannot learn through conventional means such as lengthy reading and hours of study
- [ ] Like the dialectical the must be engaged before they will respond
- [ ] Is more interested in learning the person than the lesson then they will seek the teacher out privately

The way to deal with this type of student is to extrapolate and use impromptu illustrations. Your ability to flow and adventure will inspire this student into a deeper appreciation of our skill. With that they will gladly learn from you.

___
___
___
___
___
___
___
___
___
___
___
___

9.2.8
THE ARGUMENTATIVE LEARNING STYLE

- [ ] Is loud
- [ ] Is intense
- [ ] Demands attention
- [ ] Is more interested in making their point than learning

The way to deal with this type of student is to control them immediately and to cut the legs out of their argument. The need for supporting detail is imperative with this student. Once you have controlled this situation you must now engage this tender ego with a nurturing type of persona.

9.2.9
THE LINGUISTIC LEARNER

- ☐ Process verbal and spoken information the best
- ☐ Good at reading, writing, listening and speaking
- ☐ Good at word games, puns, rhymes and tongue twisters
- ☐ Good at drama and speeches
- ☐ Thorough note takers
- ☐ Learn well from old tests
- ☐ Do well with use acronym mnemonics to help in recall

9.2.10
THE NATURALIST LEARNER

- [ ] "Process information best when it is related to finding patterns in nature and applying scientific reasoning to the understanding of living creatures"
- [ ] Environmentally motivated
- [ ] Prefer outdoors
- [ ] Like to observe nature
- [ ] They like to observe and record data

9.2.11
THE AUDITORY LEARNING STYLE

- ☐ "The auditory (musical) learner thinks in sounds rather than images"
- ☐ Chronological thinking
- ☐ Adapt better to step-by-step methods
- ☐ Remember spoken date well
- ☐ Strong language skills
- ☐ Musical ability
- ☐ Do not do well with non-verbal communication
- ☐ Do not do well with complex logic and graphic data
- ☐ Tend to read aloud

9.2.12
THE KINESTHETIC LEARNING STYLE

- ☐ Tactical learners
- ☐ Like to be physically involved in learning process
- ☐ Prefer larges spaces
- ☐ Like to draw and write
- ☐ Spontaneous
- ☐ Love hands-on lessons

9.2.13
THE VISUAL OR SPATIAL LEARNING STYLE

☐ Good at deciphering visual data in the form of maps and graphs
☐ Not good with arithmetic and numbers
☐ Not good in reading and writing
☐ Imaginative
☐ Better at process visual data versus auditory information

☐ Responds well to charts, graphs, maps, diagrams, time lines and infographics
☐ Work well with technology visual learning aids
☐ Responds well to colors
☐ Implement digital tools and technology to assist learning
☐ Highlight important points (colors or pictures)

_____
_____
_____
_____
_____
_____
_____
_____
_____
_____
_____
_____
_____
_____

9.2.14
THE LOGICAL OR MATHEMATICAL LEARNING STYLE

- [ ] Performs well in mathematics, logic, and reason
- [ ] They do well with problems involving numbers
- [ ] Can decipher abstract visual information
- [ ] Skilled at analysis
- [ ] Prefer to categorize data into agendas, tables and charts
- [ ] Perform hard complex strategy games
- [ ] They try to understand the lesson rather than memorize
- [ ] Can adapt material and lessons into games

9.2.15
INTERPERSONAL LEARNING STYLE

- ☐ Not interested in opinion, factual and verifiable information moves them
- ☐ Validates credentials, knowledge and skill
- ☐ Not interested in the conversion, only interested proof of the subject matter

9.2.16
INTRAPERSONAL LEARNING STYLE

- [ ] Focuses on only one thing at a time
- [ ] Your feeling on topic greatly influence the way you approach solution
- [ ] Feelings play a large part in determining the success of the project

9.2.17
APOLOGETIC LEARNING STYLE

- [ ] Not interested in opinion, factual and verifiable information moves them
- [ ] Validates credentials, knowledge and skill
- [ ] Not interested in the conversion, only interested proof of the subject matter

9.2.18
THE EXPLORATION LEARNING STYLE

- ☐ Creates unique methods to solve problems.
- ☐ Prone to move at their own pace
- ☐ Confident prone to arrogance
- ☐ Over confidence develops arrogance

9.2.19
THE CONFRONTATIONAL LEARNING STYLE

- ☐ Accommodating
- ☐ Avoiding
- ☐ Collaborating
- ☐ Competitive
- ☐ Uncompromising
- ☐ Argumentative and boisterous

9.2.20
THE TESTIMONIAL LEARNING STYLE

- ☐ Clear communicator
- ☐ Active listener
- ☐ Transparent about personal life
- ☐ Loves to tell their story

9.2.21
THE RECIPROCAL LEARNING STYLE

- ☐ Likes setting distinct goals and benchmarks
- ☐ Functions best in a performance-based environment
- ☐ Encourages input and feedback from the audience

9.2.22
THE TASK LEARNING STYLE

- ☐ Prefers task and quantifiable data
- ☐ Works best when there are achievable objectives
- ☐ Encouraged by decision-making and team building through individual contribution

9.2.23
THE PROBLEM-SOLVING LEARNING STYLE

- ☐ Likes simple clear goals
- ☐ Likes fluidity and freedom of movement and growth
- ☐ Looks at ministry issues from a cause and result perspective
- ☐ Likes freedom to be adaptive as problem

9.2.24
THE INVITATIONAL LEARNING STYLE

- ☐ Hospitable
- ☐ Persuasive
- ☐ Outgoing
- ☐ Energetic
- ☐ Driven
- ☐ Enthusiastic

9.2.25
THE SERVICE LEARNING STYLE

- ☐ Likes working unnoticed
- ☐ Prefer to serve in programs than teach
- ☐ Not prone to non-personal ministry growth
- ☐ Make diligent church laity
- ☐ Service traded for teaching

9.2.26
COMMAND LEARNING STYLE[55]

- [ ] Controls pace of learning
- [ ] Quarrelsome and reluctant to relinquish their belief system
- [ ] Must be bested to be open to the teacher
- [ ] Believe teacher has too much control

9.2.27
PRACTICAL LEARNING STYLE

- [ ] Likes touch learning
- [ ] Believes in doing first thing first
- [ ] Advances slowly, because of their cautious nature

9.2.28
GUIDED DISCOVERY LEARNING STYLE

- [ ] Quick and easily motivated
- [ ] Likes problem solving
- [ ] Likes following
- [ ] Believes in discipleship

9.2.29
THE ATHEIST [5657]

The fool hath said in his heart, there is no God. They are corrupt, they have done abominable works, *there is* none that doeth good Psalms 14:1

    Before we investigate how to witness to Atheists, let us take a look and a definition and some common traits[58] of this peculiar group. Traditionally an Atheist is one that does not believe in God or gods. However, this s not accurate. The term itself holds two parts, 'A' Greek for without and Theos meaning God or Spiritual Knowledge. Consequently, Atheists are people who are without a God and or have no Spiritual Knowledge. There are therefore lost by scriptural definition.

    Despite their seeming hostility towards things of God, they do not hate Him they simply have found no use for Him or are disappointed in Him blaming Him for some life event, or thirdly, they have been turned off by his representatives.

- ☐ Atheists, in general, are more likely to be younger males
- ☐ Atheists also are more likely to be white
- ☐ Atheists tent to be highly educated
- ☐ Atheists overwhelmingly favor same-sex marriage
- ☐ They support legal abortion
- ☐ The majority feel that government aid to the poor does not help
- ☐ Many believe in God but not organized religion of Christianity
- ☐ Virtually no atheists turn to religion for guidance on questions of right and wrong
- ☐ Many rely on science for guidance on questions of right and wrong
- ☐ Many Atheists find their religion on 'practical experience and common sense' as
- ☐ Most atheists believe it is not necessary to believe in God to be moral

_____
_____
_____

9.2.29.1 METHODS SUGGESTED IN DEALING WITH ATHEISTS, OR CYNICS

9.2.29.1 Judgmentalism always works against ministry, but with atheist it serves to confirm their view of the church

9.2.29.2 They are the mission, clinical dispassionate ministry also serves to confirm their view of the church

9.2.29.3 Be sincere in your empathy and compassion

9.2.29.4 Demonstrate a humble, forgiving, loving spirit; but do not patronize

9.2.29.5 Do not take rejection personally (this applies to everything in ministry)

9.2.29.2 REASONS SUGGESTED FOR FAILURE IN DEALING WITH ATHEISTS, OR CYNICS

9.2.29.2.1 Spending time judging their lifestyle and calling them sinners instead of being kind to the lost. By judging them sinners, and holding this against them, we damage the witness, and do harm to them because they will resent the church and is ministers.

9.2.29.2.2 The dumbest thing to say to a person is that it happened to me too, and o got over it. No one that is hurting cares to have salt thrown in their wounds, or their pain trivialized.

9.2.29.2.3 Their pain is as real as ours was or is, they are NOT THE ENEMY, Jesus died for them as well, and we must remember there is no call to judge the lost, minimize their hurt or sell them fairy tales of Gods power. Lying to them about God's movements and what He will do or them cause crisis of faith within the church, it chases away those lost trying to find Him. Their anger boils when He does not do some of the clichés church sells.

9.2.31.2.4 Be prepared to answer questions about anything including corruption in the church. DO NOT discuss Bible authorship as corruption, this is a favorite attack. There is undoubtedly corruption in the church, to disavow or not acknowledge is another hole in ministry. How can we judge them as sinners but hold on to and defend the sin within the church?

9.2.31.2.5 Do not be preachy or tacky in the approach, wait for them to open dialogue. Look for open ended questions like why you are a believer, or why do you feed, or go on mission trips, or what do you think about gay marriage etc. Once they have opened the door, feel free to walk through.

9.2.31.2.6 While I am not a proponent of taking everyone to the house (2 John 1:11, 2 John 7-11), and inviting to church no longer works very well. I advocate coffee shops and places where you can relax and talk or even get loud argue and laugh. We are not going to win a soul without winning the person.

10.0 THE TEACHER'S ASSESSMENT CENTER

"**Study to shew thyself approved unto God, a workman that needeth not to be ashamed, rightly dividing the word of truth**," - (2 Timothy 2:15).

10.1
TEACHING STYLES

- Dynamic Style
- Dialectical Style
- Didactic Style
- Demonstrative Style
- Animated Style
- Empirical Style
- Abstract Style
- Argumentative Style
- Command Style
- Practical Style
- Reciprocal Style

- Task Style
- Guided Discovery Style
- Problem-Solving Style
- Exploration Style
- Apologetic Style
- Confrontational Style
- Testimonial Style
- Interpersonal Style
- Invitational Style
- Service Style

According to the Center for Teaching Excellence, "Developing an effective teaching style for your subject area needs time, effort, a willingness to experiment with different teaching strategies and an examination of what is effective in your teaching[59]."

The Center also suggests that a teacher;
1. Should not try to mimic favorite teachers from the past, their effect yes, not necessarily imitative but analytically
2. Should consider their own strengths and develop them
3. Develop comfortable approaches
4. Encourage student engagement

Further; the Center reminds us that students have distinctive styles of learning. Studies show that students absorb and remember information in diverse ways, at different speeds and volume. A good teacher must familiarize themselves with learning style differences, this analysis often aids in the development of teaching styles.

Conflicts between learning and teaching styles are the most common cause of learning impairment. Be all things to all men is God's[60] admonishing to manage our teaching styles develop them within the framework of John 3:16.

According to *Study.com*, "…a speaker's style is simply the unique way in which the information is delivered to the audience[61]." Speaking (vocal-teaching) styles complete our compendium of teaching styles, comprising a grand total of #21.

Either method vocal or written teaching styles and prep methods are practical and valid, but improper use of preparation can invalidate them easily and undermine the entire purpose of the gathering which to learn about and grow closer to God.

In furtherance of our awareness and analysis of our efficacy, we delve into the teaching styles; their strengths and weakness and how they affect the Gospel.

10.1.2
THE DYNAMIC STYLE

DYNAMIC - A dynamic speaker is one that is full of energy. A dynamic style is one that is overflowing with understandable, useful information.

- ☐ Comprised of energy or relating to energy or objects in motion
- ☐ Energy in teaching
- ☐ Let the lesson speak for itself
- ☐ Let the information be the focal point
- ☐ Relating to the study of dynamics
- ☐ Learn which dynamics are effective for your style and your personality
- ☐ Characterized by continuous change, activity, or progress
- ☐ Continuous change
- ☐ Activity
- ☐ Progress
- ☐ Marked by intensity, vigor, forcefulness
- ☐ Excitement
- ☐ Confidence
- ☐ Manifested in dynamics
- ☐ Relating to variation of intensity
- ☐ Voice inflection
- ☐ Tone
- ☐ Pitch
- ☐ An interactive system or process, especially one involving competing or conflicting forces
- ☐ Often referred to as the Devil's advocate
- ☐ Feed forward
- ☐ Feed back

_____
_____
_____
_____
_____
_____
_____

10.1.3
THE DIALECTICAL STYLE

DIALECTICAL - The art of this style relies on communication skills and the Speaker's repertoire of supporting information. This style is more academic and breeds thinkers, debaters and this method teaches by the exchange of logical arguments. The process consists of:

- [ ] Stating a thesis
- [ ] Developing a contradictory thesis
- [ ] Synthesizing both theses
- [ ] This method thrives on the symbiotic relationship between opposing forces. Here the two forces transform into a new theory which then exists alone in its new harmony
- [ ] Spoken process
- [ ] Use the tools of your trade to get the message across
- [ ] Systematic weighing of contradictory facts to the resolution of their contradictions
- [ ] Contradiction
- [ ] Not a revolutionary method, simply a disagreement
- [ ] Yin and Yang - The contradiction between two conflicting forces viewed as the determining factor in their continuing interaction
- [ ] Brings about harmony and balance

_____
_____
_____
_____
_____
_____
_____
_____

10.1.4
THE DIDACTIC STYLE

DIDACTIC - A didactic or poets style is simple yet effective. It relies on the discourse of the speaker in a delivery of a simple methodology to covey the lesson.

- [ ] The Didactic system operates by instructing in a simply and straight forward manner. It relies on the personality of the instructor to convey the lesson.
- [ ] Intended to instruct.
- [ ] Simple
- [ ] Informative
- [ ] Morally instructive.
- [ ] Not a hustle, the simple facts
- [ ] Nothing added to it
- [ ] *Sine-cere* - without wax
- [ ] Inclined to teach or moralize excessively
- [ ] Tact is necessary
- [ ] More theoretical than practical application
- [ ] No real animation

_____
_____
_____
_____
_____
_____
_____
_____
_____
_____

10.1.5
THE DEMONSTRATIVE STYLE

DEMONSTRATIVE - A highly visual style that relies on simple illustrations to illustrate points and theories. Although these illustrations are easy to understand lessons cost and functionality limit the number and vividness of examples. Deriving from the belief that overly emotional and expressive people acted thusly because they were possessed by demons. This style relies mostly on the use of actions and physical demonstrations.

☐ Serving to manifest or prove
☐ Overt, physical actions
☐ Involving or characterized by demonstration
☐ Colorful descriptive terms

☐ Marked by open expression of emotion
☐ Use of emotion to indicate truth
☐ Use of emotional grammar
☐ Relies on emotional persuasion to make points (Emoting)

_____
_____
_____
_____
_____
_____
_____
_____
_____
_____
_____
_____

10.1.6
THE ANIMATED STYLE

ANIMATED - The animated style requires less of the demonstrative use of illustrations and more on the animation of the instructor. The instructor uses acts, comedy, and pantomime to enliven and make the lesson more learnable.

- ☐ To give life to; fill with life
- ☐ To energize
- ☐ To move, in motion
- ☐ To enliven
- ☐ To inspire
- ☐ To fill with spirit, courage, or resolution; encourage
- ☐ To breathe life into
- ☐ To inspire to action; prompt
- ☐ To impart motion or activity to
- ☐ To give of yourself
- ☐ To foster movement in another person
- ☐ Uses the illusion of motion

_____
_____
_____
_____
_____
_____
_____
_____
_____
_____
_____
_____
_____
_____
_____

10.1.7
THE EMPIRICAL STYLE

EMPIRICAL - Both this style and his instructor are usually boring, mechanical, and monotonous. This is a difficult style to master and usually is utilized for the more technical subjects.

- ☐ Relying on or derived from observation or experiment: Empirical results that supported the hypothesis
- ☐ Often uses scientific methods to create a lesson
- ☐ Verifiable or provable by observation or experiment: empirical laws
- ☐ Practical application
- ☐ Guided by practical experience and not theory

10.1.8
THE ABSTRACT STYLE

ABSTRACT - This style is altruistic in nature and its proponents were once considered, 'Flower children'. This style is used mostly for concepts like love, eternity, or unverifiable theories.

- ☐ Considered separate from the norm or absolute.
- ☐ Theories and schemata are usually introduced this way
- ☐ Difficult to grasp because it is often in the Speaker's head
- ☐ Not easily understood
- ☐ Without reference, practical application, or proof

10.1.09
THE ARGUMENTATIVE STYLE

ARGUMENTATIVE - A style devoted to proving a perspective or changing a view. This style relies less on teaching and more on the instructor's ability to influence the listener.

- [ ] A course of reasoning aimed at proving the truth or falsehood of something
- [ ] Offered as proof or disproof of a statement
- [ ] Used most often in moral debates and humanistic teaching

10.1.10
THE COMMAND STYLE

COMMAND - With this style teachers give demonstrations of the expected performance, as well as emphasize and explain specific important points of the lesson.

- ☐ The demonstration gives the students an opportunity to see the skill performed accurately
- ☐ Observe the critical elements of the task.
- ☐ The teacher may guide the class through the various steps in carrying out the task.
- ☐ The students repeat the performance under supervision many times as they put the movements together in the proper sequence and timing.
- ☐ Concise path to the goal, developing a clear method for attaining the desired result.

_____
_____
_____
_____
_____
_____
_____
_____
_____
_____
_____
_____
_____
_____

10.1.11
THE PRACTICAL STYLE

PRACTICAL - predicated with a demonstration and description of what is to be achieved.

- [ ] Encourages apprentice and discipleship
- [ ] Based heavily on the apprenticeship model of watch and work with the teacher and learn from real life application.
- [ ] The command style does not encourage much decision making by the student.
- [ ] Explains the methodology, when, and why it is used
- [ ] Describing the fundamentals
- [ ] The senior watches and makes corrections and provides encouragement.
- [ ] Concise path to the objective, developing a clear method for attaining the desired result.

10.1.12
THE RECIPROCAL STYLE

RECIPROCAL - style allows more decision making by the students as compared to the command and practice styles, which are much more teacher dominated.

☐ The teacher sets out goals and benchmarks

☐ The task sets also include lessons learned as a set of guidelines

☐ This style relies heavily on poling the audience before during and after, while the student listens to their critique of their product.

10.1.13
THE TASK STYLE

TASK - style is a modular format, allowing growth and development along predetermined lines, but at that student's pace.

- ☐ Requires the teacher to determine the actual level of the student and start the task at that point.
- ☐ As the lessons progress, the teacher should increase both the level of difficulty, and the level of independence of the student.
- ☐ At higher levels the skills and the decision-making requirements of the student, an emphasis team building through individual contribution.

10.1.14
THE GUIDED DISCOVERY STYLE

GUIDED DISCOVERY - This approach requires the teacher to set guidelines and goals, but there is some input in the individual method use to attain the goal.

☐ This method allows students to discover new methods to achieve the goals

☐ This method encourages students to decide how they will mature

☐ Teachers impose guidelines that limit the choices for the student's safety and benefit.

☐ This method allows the student to learn how to adapt their style to work in conjunction with other styles.

___
___
___
___
___
___
___
___
___
___
___
___
___
___
___

10.1.15
THE PROBLEM-SOLVING STYLE

PROBLEM SOLVING - This approach requires the teacher to set guidelines and goals, but there is little input in the individual method use to attain the goal.

- [ ] This method allows students to discover multiple methods to achieve the goals
- [ ] This method encourages students to decide how they will mature
- [ ] Teachers instruct in parameters only, to make sure the student does not cross the boundaries of the faith.
- [ ] This method allows the student to learn how to adapt their style to work in conjunction with other styles.
- [ ] The objectives in this style can be accomplished in many different solutions, and the student is encouraged to explore them all.
- [ ] Students develop more finesse as they watch the methods manifest.
- [ ] This style helps develop problem solving skills, and creativity.

_____
_____
_____
_____
_____
_____
_____
_____
_____
_____

10.1.16
THE EXPLORATION STYLE

EXPLORATION style - This style is useful for introducing concepts, ideas, and new equipment

☐ Fosters unique methods to solve problems.

☐ Student has more freedom of input and can also move at their own pace.

☐ This method builds confidence more quickly.

_____
_____
_____
_____
_____
_____
_____
_____
_____
_____
_____
_____
_____
_____
_____
_____
_____

10.1.17
THE CONFRONTATIONAL STYLE

CONFRONTATIONAL - Often referred to as 'Contact' or 'Cold Call' This is most often personal and small group scenario. Unlike proclamation, this is not decree or verbose but a more intimate encounter.

☐ Everyone is an opportunity
☐ Confident

☐ Must be well versed and able to handle rejection and hostility

10.1.18
THE TESTIMONIAL STYLE

TESTIMONIAL - Testimonial style develops systematic and team orientation. This assembly line format focuses on the biblical format of sowing, watering, and reaping.

- ☐ Clear communication
- ☐ Active listening
- ☐ Makes examples of personal life, ups and downs
- ☐ Openly share the account of how God reached you
- ☐ Empathy due to similarity between personal experience and the other peoples
- ☐ Compassion develops from experience

_____
_____
_____
_____
_____
_____
_____
_____
_____
_____
_____
_____
_____
_____

10.1.19
THE INTERPERSONAL STYLE

INTERPERSONAL - This is community and small group informal interaction based. This relies heavily on the amiability of the deliverer.

☐ Clear message
☐ More determined and planned approach
☐ Emphasis placed on developing communication skills
☐ Use of nonverbal communication includes body language, gestures and facial expressions
Active listening

☐ Corroboration and confirmation of understanding of delivered message is a hallmark
☐ Active listening

_____
_____
_____
_____
_____
_____
_____
_____
_____
_____
_____
_____
_____

10.1.20
THE INVITATIONAL STYLE

INVITATIONAL - This method also relies on amiability of the deliverer. This style relies heavily on a church base to invite people to.

- ☐ Hospitable
- ☐ Persuasive
- ☐ Outgoing
- ☐ Energetic
- ☐ Driven
- ☐ Enthusiastic
- ☐ Spiritually opportunistic

10.1.21
THE SERVICE STYLE

SERVICE - Often viewed as mission work. Feeding and clothing people is a successful way to make inroads and a difference in the lives of everyone encountered even without conversion. Service's greatest effect is in remining all that see it of the love of God.

- ☐ Results driven
- ☐ More personal service and interaction than teaching
- ☐ Makes service the inroad and allows for a lot more compassion and humility
- ☐ Makes the whole person the mission

10.1.22
THE APOLOGETIC STYLE

APOLOGETIC - Apologetics is the process of defending the faith through systematic argumentations and discourse. Apologetics is always technical when done correctly because it closes the doors on critics as it moves. This style always attracts and repels simultaneously for the true apologist comes off as a know it all.

- [ ] Evidential apologetics
- [ ] Historical evidence
- [ ] Archeological evidence
- [ ] Classical evidence
- [ ] Scriptural evidence
- [ ] Requires a wide base of study

10.2 STRENGTHS AND WEAKNESSES OF THE TEACHING STYLES

- Dynamic Style
- Dialectical Style
- Didactic Style
- Demonstrative Style
- Animated Style
- Empirical Style
- Abstract Style
- Argumentative Style
- Command Style
- Practical Style
- Reciprocal Style

- Task Style
- Guided Discovery Style
- Problem-Solving Style
- Exploration Style
- Apologetic Style
- Confrontational Style
- Testimonial Style
- Interpersonal Style
- Invitational Style
- Service Style

In martial arts there is no best style, each style has its strengths and weaknesses. Though these components are neither good nor bad they allow each teacher a way to prevail or equal the other styles. The determination of your style should not be predicated upon what you want but what you are. For example, a person that stands five feet tall may well take Tai-Kwon-Do but they will have an arduous time making contact with a person standing a foot taller. This inequity is not caused by failure on the shorter person's part but by the physical make up of each opponent. Ju-jitsu is a far better suited style for a shorter person. Ground fighting nullifies the advantage the taller person has over the shorter.

In much the same manner each of us has two teaching styles; the one we prefer and the one we are best at. As teachers our object is to be effective, so we should use the style best suited to us. As it is with teachers in the correct style, the elements of the style will invariably help us overcome the obstacles found in teaching.

10.2.1
THE DYNAMIC STYLE

STRENGTHS

- ☐ Agreeable
- ☐ Understandable
- ☐ Allows speaker to relax
- ☐ Takes focus off the words, breaks up the monotony

WEAKNESSES

- ☐ Gives the impression of knowledge
- ☐ Appears to lack preparation
- ☐ Not that informative
- ☐ Distracting

Not that informative

10.2.2
DIALECTICAL STYLE

STRENGTHS

- ☐ Keeps people's attention confrontation
- ☐ Encourages exchange of information Preparation
- ☐ Encourages people to think

WEAKNESSES

- ☐ Brings forth
- ☐ Requires a lot of
- ☐ Difficult to control
- ☐ People consider this style too complicated

10.2.3
THE DIDACTIC STYLE

STRENGTHS

- [ ] Issues are Black and White
- [ ] Appearing to be Truth
- [ ] Clarity
- [ ] Easy to defend

WEAKNESSES

- [ ] Not taken seriously
- [ ] Bland
- [ ] Overly simple

10.2.4
DEMONSTRATIVE STYLE

STRENGTHS
- ☐ Clarity
- ☐ Confidence
- ☐ Keeps attention
- ☐ Often lacks scope

WEAKNESSES
- ☐ Makes learning fun
- ☐ Distracting
- ☐ Lack of confidence
- ☐ Prone to comedic overtures

10.2.5
THE ANIMATED STYLE

STRENGTHS

- ☐ Keeps attention
- ☐ Distracting
- ☐ Energizing
- ☐ Doesn't require proof
- ☐ Encouraging

WEAKNESSES

- ☐ Not often taken seriously
- ☐ Makes environment
- ☐ People usually remember the light-hearted animation more

10.2.6
THE EMPIRICAL STYLE

STRENGTHS

- ☐ Obvious and plain
- ☐ Difficult to refute
- ☐ Requires in depth study of surrounding issues
- ☐ Not always correct

WEAKNESSES

- ☐ Can be contradicted by facts or science
- ☐ Always obvious
- ☐ Requires opponents to do their homework

_____
_____
_____
_____
_____
_____
_____
_____
_____
_____
_____
_____
_____
_____
_____
_____
_____

10.2.7
ABSTRACT STYLE

STRENGTHS

- ☐ Freedom to be open and frank
- ☐ Few if any preexisting prejudices
- ☐ You always seem cutting edge

WEAKNESSES

- ☐ Without pre-existing acceptance of the speaker trying to convince of latest ideas proves difficult
- ☐ Proof is often not forthcoming
- ☐ Relies too much on rhetoric and conjecture because there is so little fact

10.2.8
THE ARGUMENTATIVE STYLE

STRENGTHS

- ☐ Allows speaker to incorporate more of their personality
- ☐ Makes room for mistakes
- ☐ Does not have to be completely proven.
- ☐ Easiest way to convince or influence
- ☐ Like most conflicts the argument constantly requires upgrades to maintain the tempo

WEAKNESSES

- ☐ In the presence of opponents this style allows for much debate and even hostility
- ☐ More intellectual persons are prone not to be moved
- ☐ The banter becomes inane after repeated attempts so not succeed

10.2.09
APOLOGETIC STYLE

STRENGTHS | **WEAKNESSES**

- ☐ Not based in opinion, factual and verifiable
- ☐ Develops teacher's base of knowledge and skill set
- ☐ Provides information for persons of any educational level

- ☐ Comes across as clinical
- ☐ Often devoid of warmth
- ☐ Leads to diatribes often which lead away from the actual ministry portion

10.2.10
THE EXPLORATION STYLE

STRENGTHS

- ☐ Fosters unique methods to solve problems
- ☐ Student has more freedom of input and can also move at their own pace
- ☐ This method builds confidence more quickly

WEAKNESSES

- ☐ Over confidence develops arrogance
- ☐ This often gives rise to novices going off center
- ☐ Often these novices develop an opinion-based system and because they are novices are allowed to continue uncorrected, as they mature

10.2.11
THE CONFRONTATIONAL STYLE

STRENGTHS	WEAKNESSES
☐ Accommodating ☐ Avoiding ☐ Collaborating ☐ Competing ☐ Compromising	☐ Argumentation and boisterous and comes across as trying to intimidate ☐ Buries problems hoping they self-resolve, creating more problems in the long run ☐ Collaborating ☐ Competing ☐ Compromising

_____
_____
_____
_____
_____
_____
_____
_____
_____
_____
_____
_____
_____
_____

10.2.12
THE TESTIMONIAL STYLE

STRENGTHS

- [ ] Clear communication
- [ ] Active listening
- [ ] Transparent about personal life
- [ ] Can develop dogma and witness about things only you find important, chasing away the target audience

WEAKNESSES

- [ ] Becomes an opportunity to boast about your sin
- [ ] Leads to judgmentalism
- [ ] People learn to find value in the teacher not the lesson of the God they teach of

10.2.13
THE RECIPROCAL STYLE

STRENGTHS   **WEAKNESSES**

- ☐ Distinct goals and benchmarks
- ☐ Helpful guidelines
- ☐ Encourages input and feedback from the audience

- ☐ The complexity of the task and the developmental level of the student are not equal
- ☐ The method can often be too advanced for students
- ☐ Time consuming

10.2.14
THE TASK STYLE

STRENGTHS

- [ ] The styles require the teacher to determine the actual level of the student and start the task at that point
- [ ] As the lessons progress, the teacher should increase both the level of difficulty, and the level of independence of the student

WEAKNESSES

- [ ] Encourages decision-making and team building through individual contribution
- [ ] Tasks often bore and drive away the new convert
- [ ] Leads to salvation by works mentality
- [ ] Impersonal and sees souls as numbers on a chart

10.2.15
THE PROBLEM-SOLVING STYLE

STRENGTHS   **WEAKNESSES**

- ☐ This method allows students to discover multiple methods to achieve the goals
- ☐ This method encourages students to decide how they will mature
- ☐ Teachers instruct in parameters only, to make sure the student does not cross the boundaries of the faith.
- ☐ This method allows the student to learn how to adapt their style to work in conjunction with other styles
- ☐ The objectives in this style can be accomplished in many different solutions, and the student is encouraged to explore them all
- ☐ Difficult to master this style as it is an evolutionary process
- ☐ Time consuming
- ☐ Requires constant monitoring from teacher else the intellect override the spirit.
- ☐ Teacher has to make sure they are able to guide the student and they do not develop arrogance

10.2.16
THE INVITATIONAL STYLE

STRENGTHS

- ☐ Hospitable
- ☐ Persuasive
- ☐ Outgoing
- ☐ Energetic
- ☐ Driven
- ☐ Enthusiastic
- ☐ Spiritually opportunistic

WEAKNESSES

- ☐ Often places students in environments to be drawn back to the darkness
- ☐ Easy to become the person that is invited away from God
- ☐ Based too much on emotion
- ☐ Depends too much on teacher ability to connect with the student

10.2.17
THE INTERPERSONAL STYLE

STRENGTHS   **WEAKNESSES**[62]

- ☐ Clear message
- ☐ More determined and planned approach
- ☐ Emphasis placed on developing communication skills
- ☐ Use of nonverbal communication includes body language, gestures and facial expressions
- ☐ Active listening

- ☐ Corroboration and confirmation of understanding of delivered message is a hallmark
- ☐ Tendency to get emotional
- ☐ Requires a lot of self-confidence
- ☐ Discouraging for those easily hurt by rejection
- ☐ Share than teach
- ☐ Tendency to try to steer rather than teach

10.2.18
THE SERVICE STYLE

STRENGTHS

- ☐ Develops humility
- ☐ Improves the reputation of the church
- ☐ Develops the giving nature of the student

WEAKNESSES

- ☐ Develops salvation by works mentality
- ☐ Service traded for prayer
- ☐ Stop talking to God and consider service the higher calling

10.2.19
COMMAND STYLE[63]

STRENGTHS   **WEAKNESSES**

- ☐ Controlled pace of learning
- ☐ Monitored practice is part of the style
- ☐ Moves along as teacher decides the level and advancement

- ☐ Teacher has too much control
- ☐ Little apprentice value as the teacher instils their edicts rather than groom

_____
_____
_____
_____
_____
_____
_____
_____
_____
_____
_____
_____
_____
_____
_____
_____
_____
_____
_____
_____

10.2.20
PRACTICAL STYLE

STRENGTHS

- ☐ Allows students to work at their own proficiency level
- ☐ This style also allows for individual feedback from the teacher

WEAKNESSES

- ☐ Student must have a basic skill set and the ability to function independently
- ☐ Without assistance, bad habits go unnoticed and un corrected

10.2.21
GUIDED DISCOVERY STYLE

STRENGTHS

- ☐ Quick and efficient way to motivate
- ☐ Encourages individual problem solving
- ☐ Individual work helps develop skill set

WEAKNESSES

- ☐ Students many not ask for help when needed
- ☐ Enables students to ride the bench and not participate if they choose to

10.3
STYLE DETERMINATION

(A lot yourself 8 minutes for this exercise.)

Read the passage then make do a presentation. Write in the book your questions, highlights, notes, and themes.

"**The proverbs of Solomon, the son of David, king of Israel: to know wisdom and instruction; to discern the words of understanding; to receive instruction in wise dealing, in righteousness, justice, and equity; to give prudence to the simple, knowledge and discretion to the young man: that the wise man may hear, and increase in learning; that the man of understanding may attain to sound counsel: to understand a proverb, and parables, the words and riddles of the wise**." (Proverbs 1:1-6).

_____
_____
_____
_____
_____
_____
_____
_____
_____
_____
_____
_____
_____
_____
_____

10.3.1
A WAY TO DETERMINE YOUR STYLE

Check all that apply to your style:

- ☐ I was distracting
- ☐ I was not that informative
- ☐ I appeared to lack preparation
- ☐ People considered me too complicated
- ☐ I brought forth confrontation
- ☐ I required a lot of preparation
- ☐ My lesson was difficult to control
- ☐ I was not taken seriously
- ☐ I was bland
- ☐ I was overly simple
- ☐ I lacked confidence
- ☐ I lacked scope
- ☐ I was prone to comedic overtures
- ☐ I did utilize proof
- ☐ People remembered the animation more
- ☐ Was contradicted by facts or science
- ☐ I was not always correct
- ☐ I required in depth study of surrounding issues
- ☐ I found myself trying to convince of new ideas proves difficult
- ☐ Proof was not forthcoming
- ☐ I relied too much on rhetoric and conjecture
- ☐ The banter became inane after repeated attempts did not succeed
- ☐ The more intellectual persons were not to moved
- ☐ I encountered hostility and much debate
- ☐ The argument constantly required upgrades to maintain the tempo

10.3.1 List which themes are important to you and why?

_____

_____

_____

10.3.2 What type of examples do you use?

10.3.3 What things did you decide to say, and which did you decide to exemplify"

10.3.4 consists of a compilation of all the style weakness. The evaluation is based on the style weakness because it is by the weakness of our styles we are remembered not the strengths. Take the following equation and apply it to the above tallies.
1. Take your list of weakness and compare them to the 11.2 weaknesses.
2. Then from the list you have the most in common with add the answers to the three independent questions.
3. Combing the totals find out which Synopsis describes you the best.
4. This is your style

10.3.2 DETERMINATION OF THE DYNAMIC STYLE

- [ ] Agreeable
- [ ] Understandable
- [ ] Allows speaker to relax
- [ ] Takes focus off the words, breaks up the monotony
- [ ] Distracting
- [ ] Gives the impression of knowledge
- [ ] Not that informative
- [ ] Appears to lack preparation

_____
_____
_____
_____
_____
_____
_____
_____
_____
_____
_____
_____
_____
_____
_____
_____
_____
_____
_____

10.3.3
DETERMINATION OF THE DIALECTICAL STYLE

- ☐ Keeps people's attention
- ☐ Encourages exchange of information
- ☐ Encourages people to think.

- ☐ People consider this style too complicated
- ☐ Brings forth confrontation
- ☐ Requires a lot of preparation
- ☐ Difficult to control

10.3.4
DETERMINATION OF THE DIDACTIC STYLE

☐ Issues are black and white
☐ Appearing to be truth
☐ Clarity
☐ Easy to defend

☐ Not taken seriously
☐ Bland
☐ Overly simple

10.3.5
DETERMINATION OF THE DEMONSTRATIVE STYLE

- [ ] Clarity
- [ ] Confidence
- [ ] Keeps attention
- [ ] Makes learning fun

- [ ] Distracting
- [ ] Lack of confidence
- [ ] Often lacks scope
- [ ] Prone to comedic overtures

10.3.6
DETERMINATION OF THE ANIMATED STYLE

- [ ] Keeps attention
- [ ] Energizing
- [ ] Encouraging
- [ ] Makes environment light-hearted
- [ ] Distracting

- [ ] Does not require proof
- [ ] Not often taken seriously
- [ ] People usually remember the animation more

10.3.7 DETERMINATION OF THE EMPIRICAL STYLE

☐ Not always correct
☐ Requires in depth study of surrounding issues
☐ Obvious and plain
☐ Supported by science
☐ Always obvious

☐ Difficult to refute
☐ Requires opposers to do their research
☐ Can be contradicted by facts or science

___
___
___
___
___
___
___
___
___
___
___
___
___
___
___
___
___
___
___
___

10.3.8
DETERMINATION OF THE ABSTRACT STYLE

- ☐ Trying to gain acceptance of your person, not the material
- ☐ Does not rely on poof
- ☐ Relies too much on rhetoric and conjecture - because there is so little fact
- ☐ No clear point, just assertions

10.3.9
DETERMINATION OF THE ARGUMENTATIVE STYLE

☐ The banter becomes inane after repeated attempts so not succeed
☐ More intellectual persons are prone not to be moved

☐ In the presence of opponents this style allows for much debate and even hostility
☐ Constantly needs upgrades to maintain the tempo

10.3.10
DETERMINATION OF THE APOLOGETIC STYLE

- [ ] Boring
- [ ] Creates appearance of arrogance
- [ ] I am a fundamentalist
- [ ] I came across as clinical
- [ ] I was devoid of warmth
- [ ] I spent a lot of time clearing up misconceptions

10.3.11
DETERMINATION OF THE EXPLORATION STYLE

- ☐ Developed unique methods to solve problems
- ☐ I felt more confidence
- ☐ I was comfortable, not arrogant
- ☐ I enjoyed exploring new horizons

10.3.12
DETERMINATION OF THE CONFRONTATIONAL STYLE

- [ ] I was too accommodating
- [ ] Ignored problems hoping they self-resolve
- [ ] Collaborating
- [ ] Competing
- [ ] Compromising
- [ ] I was argumentative and boisterous and comes across as trying to intimidate

_____
_____
_____
_____
_____
_____
_____
_____
_____
_____
_____
_____
_____
_____
_____
_____
_____
_____
_____
_____

10.3.13
DETERMINATION OF THE TESTIMONIAL STYLE

- [ ] Clear communication
- [ ] I used active listening
- [ ] I was open and transparent about my personal life
- [ ] I found myself boasting about past sin
- [ ] I was judgmental
- [ ] Most of the questions were about me not God

10.3.14
DETERMINATION OF THE RECIPROCAL STYLE

- ☐ I set goals and benchmarks
- ☐ I used helpful guidelines
- ☐ I encouraged input and feedback
- ☐ I got bored
- ☐ The students frustrated me

10.3.15
DETERMINATION OF THE TASK STYLE

- [ ] I encouraged decision-making and team building through individual contribution
- [ ] I often bore and drive away the new convert
- [ ] I am saddened by small numbers of people
- [ ] I am proud when people accept Christ on my watch

10.3.16
DETERMINATION OF THE PROBLEM-SOLVING STYLE

- ☐ I encourage the student to learn how to adapt their style to work in conjunction with other styles
- ☐ I encourage students to explore all solutions
- ☐ I cannot spend enough time with each student
- ☐ I rather solution that restoring people
- ☐ I feel like a baby sitter

10.3.17
DETERMINATION OF THE INVITATIONAL STYLE

☐ I am spiritually opportunistic
☐ I often place students in environments to be drawn back to the darkness
☐ I find myself drawn easily to become the person that is invited away from God

☐ Spiritually opportunistic
☐ I'm often too much on emotion
☐ Easy to become the person that is invited away from God
☐ Based too much on emotion

10.3.18
DETERMINATION OF THE INTERPERSONAL STYLE

- ☐ I focus more on the delivery than the message
- ☐ I use nonverbal communication including body language, gestures and facial expressions
- ☐ I prefer to share rather than teach
- ☐ I have a tendency to try to steer rather than teach

10.3.19
DETERMINATION OF THE INTRAPERSONAL STYLE

- ☐ Usually a lone wolf
- ☐ I am determined to resolve issues alone
- ☐ Use of nonverbal communication
- Active listener

- ☐ Tendency to get emotional
- ☐ Active listener

_____
_____
_____
_____
_____
_____
_____
_____
_____
_____
_____
_____
_____
_____
_____
_____
_____
_____

10.3.20
THE SERVICE STYLE

- [ ] Makes me feel useful
- [ ] I like improving the reputation of Christians
- [ ] Feeds my giving nature
- [ ] I believe in salvation by works
- [ ] I tend to trade service for prayer

10.3.21
COMMAND STYLE

- [ ] I like to control the pace of learning
- [ ] I like being in control
- [ ] I do not care if they like me
- [ ] I tend to instill edicts rather than groom
- [ ] I make sure others are growing the right way

10.3.22
PRACTICAL STYLE

- [ ] I prefer to allow students to work at their own proficiency level
- [ ] I like to give feedback
- [ ] I determine the student's basic skill set and the ability to function independently
- [ ] Without my help, I believe bad habits go unnoticed and uncorrected.

10.3.23
GUIDED DISCOVERY STYLE

- [ ] I like to motivate people
- [ ] I like to help those who do cannot ask
- [ ] I encourage individual problem solving
- [ ] People that do want not to participate are free to leave

_____
_____
_____
_____
_____
_____
_____
_____
_____
_____
_____
_____
_____
_____
_____
_____
_____
_____
_____
_____
_____
_____
_____

10.4
COMMON TEACHING MISTAKES[64]

Teachers make mistakes, it is impossible to teach all the various learning styles and not make mistakes. One of the most common causes of these mistakes is not learning from previous and collective errors.

During my Project management training, I learned about a phase called 'Lessons Learned'. According to PMI (Project Management Institute) lessons learned is one of the most important and value added" aspects of the project management lifecycle[65]'. The reasons they cite for this process being so important are;

1. Fosters analysis.
2. Prevents repetition of mistakes.
3. Fosters exploration and boundary spanning.
4. Utilizes dialectical analysis.
5. Problem solving information and development.
6. Allows input from outside sources not commonly involved in internal process.

Following the Project Management Model well look at a listing from the Educational Community about lessons learned;

10.4.1 Lacking professional variety - No one wants likes boredom or listen to rehashed materials.

10.4.2 Promising something and not delivering - The 'wolf tickets' the church universal sells. Nothing creates a crisis of faith like trusting God for things and He does not deliver. Problem is when we promise things God is not responsible for we destroy Christian lives.

10.4.3 Always standing behind the lectern - Move around, standing still bores the audience and the presenter, and minimizes the effectiveness of color and any other teaching tool employed.

10.4.4 Lacking knowledge and preparation - Read the material, use bench- marks, look prepared. Presenting confidence, and fluidity is important when you are trying to convince people to change the way they think.

10.4.5 Failing to see the influence of Cultural Imperialism - Not taking culture into consideration. The word may not change, but the world has. We do not change the truth, but the delivery systems may need to be updated.

10.4.6 Not having your facts straight - Not know every answer is fine, not knowing how to find the answer of field the question is not. The student comes to learn, teachers should be prepared on collateral subjects contained in their lesson. Anything you mention in a lesson you should be able to support.

10.4.7 Talking too much and doing too much - encourage the audience to read and present study materials for clarification.

10.4.8 Relying too much on all the current pedagogical advice - Tradition and doctrine often override our teaching styles. The gifts given were given to make our approach easy for us and appealing to the student. Stiff, legalistic, unyielding tutelage is ineffective today because of the internet.

10.4.9 Talking to the board - Always face the audience, eye contact is key to sincerity and convincing.

10.4.10 Creating a shoddy or formulaic syllabus - keep it short, simple, direct, to the point.

10.4.11 Using a student to show something negative - Do not use the students as fodder. Make them part of the class, but not the brunt of disdain.

10.4.3 Failing to develop credibility - Do not put yourself down. If you have no confidence, then you cannot instill confidence.

10.4.13 Underestimating students - Students also have input, they have questions. Their questions foster dialogue.

10.4.14 In writing or composition, talking about the form before you talk about the message, or worse, never talking about the message at all - Show interest in the topic presented. If they speak about problems as about the current situation.

10.4.15 Making a course so easy that almost no learning takes place - Do not dumb it down to the point where you change the message. Worst case scenario; break down the morsels of truth into tiny pieces, but it still needs to be God's truth.

10.4.16 Taking it personally - Do not take questions as challenges. We are trying to change people's thinking, they are going to have push back; why would we not expect this uncertainty.

10.4.17 Trying to teach content without teaching the learning skills that would be helpful to the student in learning the content - We can teach truth forever, students also need aid to determine how best to apply the truth in their lives.

10.4.18 Not showing enthusiasm for your topic - Despite one of the most popular writers and pastors today's presentation; the dull unenthusiastic approach chases people away. The life should create interest and intrigue, and yes excitement.

10.4.19 Underestimating the importance of quality academic time spent with students outside - When you can answer questions in the parking lot, or via email. Sheep begat sheep. Well informed sheep are more confident and will generate interest amongst other sheep.

10.4.20 Not explaining terminology inherent to academia - Stop using big words, unless you break them down. Be sure, you use and teach word study tools.

10.04.21 Being disorganized – Be on time and consistent.

10.04.22 Lacking understanding of or interest in the academic preparedness of each student - Be prepared for the student that knows as much as you do or is at least highly prepared.

10.4.23 Telling your students - Do not patronize or trivialize your teaching, the lesson or the student.

10.4.24 Not knowing every student's name by the second week of class - My personal shortcoming. I do not understand this one personally, but it appears that many are just as dependent on their relationship with the instructor as they are the lesson.

10.4.25 Telling students they must read the textbook or other materials and then not following up on that requirement - Draw heavily on the text in classroom settings, to encourage reading. Students do not want people to know they put no effort into their study, or their own life, it is embarrassing.

10.4.26 Not setting high enough goals / expecting too little from the students - Expect growth and drive growth by coaching, exhorting, and guidance. Do not expect them to fail, if they do often it is a teaching weakness because we fail to properly motivate the student.

10.4.27 Not giving clear explanations - Make sure to explain the scriptures and the lessons as though the class is all novice. Do not spoon feed, teach.

10.4.28 Testing for knowledge and understanding of course content through limited means - Vary testing procedures from written to oral testing. Call them up to the board when you can let them learn to express themselves.

10.4.29 Not giving feedback often enough/quickly enough - Keep pace with your students. That is what computers, deacon, and elders are for, team work saves time.

10.4.30 Teaching the course material rather than teaching students - If the students do not get the information, then pushing forward benefits no one. The lesson is for the student, not the students for the lesson.

10.4.31 Failing to establish yourself as a credible source - You are the teacher; therefore, you are a credible source, otherwise why stand before them crowd and teach?

10.4.32 Adopting a new strategy just because it is popular, or everybody is doing it, without thinking it through as to whether you really are committed to that strategy - Do not be tossed to and fro by every new doctrine or policy which comes around.

10.4.33 Making a hard and fast deadline for every major assignment and allowing no make-up or extra-credit alternatives to meeting course objectives - Be flexible with the students, their time is precious too. Be sensitive to their grown patterns and learning styles.

10.4.34 Failing to allow enough time for discussion, exploration, practice, and innovation for students while they are discovering/learning a new skill or revisiting an old skill - A lot enough time in the lesson for Q&A and growth.

10.4.35 Telling students you do not care - If you say you do not care if they read or show up, then they will believe that you do not care about their souls.

10.4.36 Practicing a 'do as I say, not as I do' philosophy - If students find us making mistakes, and we try to cover them up, they lose all respect for your authority and your witness.

10.4.37 Asking a closed-ended question and then having students try to guess the exact wording of the answer you are looking for - leading is one thing, funneling makes the student feel ill equipped. However, in terms of scriptures we must expect them to know what the text books says, for many problems addressed in the bible there is only one answer, though it exists in several places.

10.4.38 Failing to give students immediate feedback on completed assignment before assigning a related task - Modular learning needs transition, be available for it or the student cannot build on the uncorrected work.

10.4.39 Not following up on the policy to correct inattentive or negative classroom behaviors - Yes, it is ok to put students out of Sunday school or church, if they are disruptive and obviously intent on curtailing the lesson, invite them to leave. Especially if they are trying to espouse unbiblical information.

10.4.40 Invalidating students' opinions and viewpoints - In terms of scriptures we must expect them to know what the text books says, for many problems addressed in the bible there is only one answer, though it may come from several places.

10.4.41 Gluing students to their chairs - Do not drag lessons out meet often but do not belabor the point.

10.4.42 Never allowing students to assess their own work - Physician heal thyself. Student grow when we turn on the lights not control the switch.

10.4.43 Making incorrect assumptions about student engagement - Trying to determine everything about a student's interest by body language, people learn differently therefore the way they earn will also have varied appearance.

10.4.44 Responding with 'You should know that' when a student asks a question - This response my hinder self-confidence.

10.4.45 Getting too familiar with your students - objectivity is a must. This is for safety as well as self-control and accountability. Someone (Elders in the church) needs to be there for check and balance purposes.

11.0 MORE EFFECTIVE LESSONS

"'Whom shall he teach knowledge? and whom shall he make to understand doctrine? them that are weaned from the milk and drawn from the breasts. For precept must be upon precept, precept upon precept; line upon line, line upon line; here a little, and there a little: For with stammering lips and another tongue will he speak to this people'. To whom he said, 'This is the rest wherewith ye may cause the weary to rest; and this is the refreshing: yet they would not hear'. But the word of the LORD was unto them precept upon precept, precept upon precept; line upon line, line upon line; here a little, and there a little; that they might go, and fall backward, and be broken, and snared, and taken - (Isaiah 28:9-13)".

11.0
HOW TO DEVELOP A PLAN

Since teaching is basically just informative public speaking, it is logical to look at some of the best ingredients of public speaking. Here is a list of #11 things each teacher should remember about their lesson (speech[66]).

- ☐ Be Memorable
- ☐ Have a Structure
- ☐ Do not Waste the Opening
- ☐ Strike the Right Ton:
- ☐ Humanize Yourself
- ☐ Repeat Yourself
- ☐ Use Transitions
- ☐ Include Theatrics
- ☐ End Strong
- ☐ Keep it Short

_____
_____
_____
_____
_____

11.0.1 Establish direction the lesson is going
☐ What is objective?

_____
_____
_____
_____

11.0.2 Determine parameters
☐ Boundaries are important; do not let the questions take you further than the other students need go
☐ The questions are not challenges all the times they can be useful

_____
_____
_____

11.0.3 Do not be too rigid
- [ ] Small mindedness is the antithesis to teaching
- [ ] Rigidity implies a lack of preparation
- [ ] Stern is fine, but the students are here to learn as much as possible
- [ ] We can accept mediocrity IT IS NOT OUR JOB TO PRODUCE IT

11.0.4 Decide on key points
- [ ] Make a key point check list and make sure you cover them all if possible.
- [ ] If it takes longer to cover a topic but the students firmly grasp the information that is ok.

11.0.5 Apply the text to your style
- [ ] Do not let the topic shape you - the topic must conform to the teacher
- [ ] Think of the topic as clay. Even though we cannot prevent clay from being clay we can mold it into whatever we want

11.0.6 What do you want the student to see?
- [ ] Be sure that you begin out with the right clay
- [ ] They must see what can be made with clay. Who made it is far less important

11.0.7 How will you take the student there?
- [ ] Decide on how you will walk the student through the journey

11.1
WRITING A PLAN

Writing lesson plans makes sure that you are addressing the requirements of the curriculum as well as the opportunity to plan how you will best address student needs. Your church, or school district may already have a template, or you can use the Lesson Plan Template[67] as you work through creating your lesson plans.

11.1.1 ☐ Structure (John 14:7)

___

11.1.2 ☐ Intuition (1 Peter 5:8)

___

11.1.3 ☐ Knowledge (Exodus 31:3)

___

11.1.4 ☐ Commitment (Luke 9:62)

11.1.5 ☐ Being Human (Acts 20:19, 1 Peter 5:5)

11.1.6 ☐ Versatility (2 Timothy 2:21)

11.1.7 ☐ Lightness (Luke 16:8)

11.1.8 ☐ Communicate effectively (Ephesians 4:29)

11.1.9 ☐ Acting Strategically (Colossians 1:28)

11.1.10 ☐ Self-Managing (2 Peter 1:5-7)

11.1.11 ☐ Setting Clear Goals and Persisting in Achieving Them (Daniel 6:26)

_____
_____
_____
_____

11.1.12 ☐ Managing Complexity (Exodus 18:16)

_____
_____
_____
_____
_____
_____
_____
_____
_____

11.1.13 ☐ Fostering Creativity and Innovation (Philippians 6:1)

_____
_____
_____
_____
_____
_____
_____

11.1.14 ☐ Team Building and Promoting Teamwork (Ephesians 4:29)

11.1.15 ☐ Creating Lasting Relationships (Amos 3:3)

11.1.16 ☐ Learning Agility (Roman 8:11)

11.2
EFFECTIVE LESSON PLAN COMPONENTS[68]

Lessons need structure to engender results. Here are 11 more components for plan structure. Remember not all of these components need be used, but at least complying with half of them should be required requisites to a successful plan.

11.2.1 Learning Goal - What is the desired outcome from the lesson

11.2.2 Resources - Cite pertinent sources used or needed and use Subject Matter Experts, whether Christian or Secular.

11.2.3 Standards - The standards for Kingdom Lessons, are the perfecting the saints.

11.2.4 Anticipatory Set - Encourage the students to ask questions and ask for guidance this helps both the students and the teacher. Many of the questions asked will be held secretly by other students.

11.2.5 Introduction - A 30,000-foot view of the lesson overviewing the lesson.

11.2.6 Direct Instruction - What actual information you plan to use

11.23.7 Guided Instruction - Find out what your students know and can do

11.23.8 Assessment - Informal way to gauge understanding.

11.23.9 Closure - summarize or wrap up their learning.

11.23.11 Differentiated Instruction - Decide where the choke points are in your delivery timeframe and adjust to the LCS.

11.4
IMPORTANCE OF COLOR AND SHAPES IN EFFECTIVE LESSON PLANS[6970]

Color is how living things make distinctions among what they see. According to experiments with lab rats placed in a paisley box versus a plain white one, the Paisley group developed far more synaptic attachments that the other. The implications were that the complex colors and patterns fostered development in the brain, required to interpret the data.

Shapes; like colors, are the tools used to discern the images we receive through our eyes. Shapes are also symbols, which is why we use them in signs and how writing came to fruition.

Understanding the reception of data, allows us to guide the environmental stimulus to make the audience more receptive. In the world, we must rely on calming gesture, and clothing or hands outs like flowers, t-shirts and fruit.

11.4.1 SETTING THE MOOD

☐ Determining the environment, or reception as in you may have to wear the colors yourself. Find subtle ways to utilize the preferred colors for that mood.

☐ A monochromatic color set up will give your presentation a feeling of harmony and comfort.

☐ Analogous color set up adds variation and is good attention grabbing and makes complicated topics easier to contend with.

☐ Complementary color set ups get attention! The is flower power at work, loud colors to keep audience off balance and focused on you.

☐ Triadic color set ups guide the eyes, and aid in relaying balance and visually captivating presentations

12.0 THE SPIRITUAL SKILLS

"Now concerning spiritual gifts, brothers, I do not want you to be uninformed. You know that when you were pagans you were led astray to mute idols; however, you were led. Therefore, I want you to understand that no one speaking in the Spirit of God ever says, 'Jesus is accursed!' and no one can say 'Jesus is Lord' except in the Holy Spirit.

Now there are varieties of gifts, but the same Spirit; and there are varieties of service, but the same Lord; and there are varieties of activities, but it is the same God who empowers them all in everyone. To each is given the manifestation of the Spirit for the common good. For to one is given through the Spirit the utterance of wisdom, and to another the utterance of knowledge according to the same Spirit, to another faith by the same Spirit, to another gifts of healing by the one Spirit, to another the working of miracles, to another prophecy, to another the ability to distinguish between spirits, to another various kinds of tongues, to another the interpretation of tongues. All these are empowered by one and the same Spirit, who apportions to each one individually as He wills." (1 Corinthians 3:1-3).

12.0
THE SPIRITUAL SKILLS

If we are going to teach about spiritual things and about the Holy Spirit, it would serve us well to if not understand at least learn what these gifts are. Part of our teaching craft will most certainly entail teaching upon or helping nurture these gifts.

Revelation 13:14 gives us another reason to teach about and nurture the gifts of the Holy Spirit. **"And deceiveth them that dwell on the earth by the means of those miracles which he had power to do in the sight of the beast; saying to them that dwell on the earth, that they should make an image to the beast, which had the wound by a sword, and did live."** How are people and students supposed to discern the truth and the deception f they have no idea about or how to develop and use their spiritual gifts.

According to scholars there are three groups of spiritual gifts[71].

- 12.1.1 **Gifts of Revelation**
    - 12.1.1.1 Word of wisdom - The application of knowledge {This is not prophecy}

    - 12.1.1.2 Word of knowledge - Receiving facts supernaturally by the Spirit {This is not prophecy}

    - 12.1.1.3 Discerning of spirits - Figuring out the source of a spirit

- 12.1.2 **Spoken Gifts**
    - 12.1.2.1 Tongues - Tongues: three

supernatural means of communication

12.1.2.1.1 - Tongues unto God (1 Corinthians 14:2)

12.1.2.1.2 - Tongues as a sign to the unbeliever (Acts 2)

12.1.2.1.3 - Tongues that edify the body of believers - (1 Corinthians 14:5)

12.1.2.1.4 Interpretation of tongues - translation of divine utterances

12.1.2.1.5 Prophecy - revelation for edification of church

12.1.3 Gifts of Power

12.1.3.1 Faith - The gift that allows us to

12.1.3.2 Healing - Restoration of health

12.1.3.3 Working of miracles - Divine actions

12.2
UNDERSTANDING THE SPIRITUAL SKILLS[72]

This assessment is based on honest answer to the questions. There is no automated method to tabulate the answer offered in this resource. Use the following key and the median answer with the highest score is most likely the area you will perform the best in, in your ministry life.

Options:
5 - Highly characteristic of me/definitely true for me
4 - Most of the time this would describe me/be true for me
3 - Frequently characteristic of me/true for me–about 50 percent of the time
2 - Occasionally characteristic of me/true for me–about 25 percent of the time
1 - Not at all characteristic of me/definitely untrue for me

The compilation of gifts is part of the Assessment Inventory complied by the adapted articles. Source citations include;
- Romans (3:6-8)
- 1 Corinthians (3:8-11)
- 1 Corinthians (28-30)
- Ephesians (4:11)
- 1 Peter (4:9-11)

12.2.1 **Leadership**[72] - Leading and directing; "**...if it is to encourage, then give encouragement; if it is giving, then give generously; if it is to lead, do it diligently; if it is to show mercy, do it cheerfully** (Romans 3:8)".

12.2.2 **Administration** - Organization and logistics; "**And God has placed in the church first of all apostles, second prophets, third teachers, then miracles, then gifts of**

healing, of helping, of guidance, and of different kinds of tongues (1 Corinthians 3:28)".

12.2.3 **Teaching** - (1 Corinthians. 3:28; "**Or ministry, let us wait on our ministering: or he that teacheth, on teaching** (Romans 3:7"; "**And he gave some, apostles; and some, prophets; and some, evangelists; and some, pastors and teachers** (Ephesians 4:11)".

12.2.4 **Knowledge** - Teaching and training (1 Corinthians 3:28).

12.2.5 **Wisdom** - Discernment (1 Corinthians 3:28).

12.2.6 **Prophecy** - Edifying the church "**Having then gifts differing according to the grace that is given to us, whether prophecy, let us prophesy according to the proportion of faith** (1 Corinthians 3:11), (Romans 3:6).

12.2.7 **Discernment** - Figuring out the true nature of a spirit or person (1 Corinthians 3:11).

12.2.8 **Exhortation** - Encouraging the saints (Romans 3:8).

12.2.9 **Shepherding** - Helping protect and steer the body (Ephesians 4:11).

12.12.10 **Faith** - The Christian principle that allows the body to believe the impossible and stay the course. "**To another faith by the same Spirit; to another the gifts of healing by the same Spirit** (1 Corinthians 3:9)".

12.2.11 **Evangelism** - The gift of spreading the word outside the church (Ephesians 4:11).

12.2.12 **Apostles** - Empowered to teach lead and correct (1 Corinthians 3:28; Ephesians 4:11).

12.2.13 **Service/Helps** - Stewardship, learn to love the work is also a gift (1 Cor. 3:28; Romans 3:7).

12.2.14 **Mercy** - The gift of compassion and gently rolled into one (Romans 3:8).

12.2.15 **Giving** - The ability and desire to share materials wealth for kingdom purposes (Romans 3:8).

12.2.16 **Hospitality** - Cordiality as a part of the body "**Use hospitality one to another without grudging** (1 Peter 4:9)".

12.3
THE SPIRITUAL SKILLS ASSESSMENT[73]

The Spiritual Skills Assessment is a relatively subjective test, which when filled out honestly can be of value to you in determining your skills, as well as learning to determine others. The test is limited however in its efficacy.

12.3.1 ☐ I have the ability to organize ideas, resources, time, and people effectively.

12.3.2 ☐ I am willing to study and prepare for the task of teaching.

12.3.3 ☐ I am able to relate the truths of God to specific situations.

12.3.4 ☐ I have a God-given ability to help others grow in their faith.

12.3.5 ☐ I possess a special ability to communicate the truth of salvation.

12.3.6 ☐ I have the ability to make critical decisions when necessary.

12.3.7 ☐ I am sensitive to the hurts of people.

12.3.8 ☐ I experience joy in meeting needs through sharing possessions.

12.3.9 ☐ I enjoy studying.

12.3.10 ☐ I have delivered God's message of warning and judgment.

12.3.11 ☐ I am able to sense the true motivation of persons and movements.
12.3.12 ☐ I have a special ability to trust God in demanding situations.
12.3.13 ☐ I have a strong desire to contribute to the establishment of new churches.
12.3.14 ☐ I take action to meet physical and practical needs rather than merely talking about or planning to help.
12.3.15 ☐ I enjoy entertaining guests in my home.
12.3.16 ☐ I can adapt my guidance to fit the maturity of those working with me.
12.3.17 ☐ I can delegate and assign meaningful work.
12.3.18 ☐ I have an ability and desire to teach.
12.3.19 ☐ I am usually able to analyze a situation correctly.
12.3.20 ☐ I have a natural tendency to encourage others.
12.3.21 ☐ I am willing to take the initiative in helping other Christians grow in their faith.
12.3.22 ☐ I have an acute awareness of the emotions of other people, such as loneliness, pain, fear, and anger.
12.3.21 ☐ I am a cheerful giver.
12.3.22 ☐ I spend time digging into facts.
12.3.23 ☐ I feel that I have a message from God to deliver to others.
12.2.24 ☐ I can recognize when a person

is genuine/honest.

12.3.25 ☐ I am a person of vision (a clear mental portrait of a preferable future given by God).

12.3.27 ☐ I am able to communicate vision in such a way that others commit to making the vision a reality.

12.3.28 ☐ I am willing to yield to God's will rather than question and waver.

12.3.29 ☐ I would like to be more active in getting the gospel to people in other lands.

12.3.30 ☐ It makes me happy to do things for people in need.

12.3.31 ☐ I am successful in getting a group to do its work joyfully. I am able to make strangers feel at ease.

12.3.32 ☐ I have the ability to plan learning approaches.

12.3.33 ☐ I can identify those who need encouragement.

12.3.34 ☐ I have trained Christians to be more obedient Disciples of Christ.

12.3.35 ☐ I am willing to do whatever it takes to see others come to Christ.

12.3.36 ☐ I am attracted to people who are hurting.

12.3.37 ☐ I am a generous giver.

12.3.38 ☐ I am able to discover new truths.

12.3.39 ☐ I have spiritual insights from Scripture concerning issues and people that compel me to speak out.

12.2.40 ☐ I can sense when a person is acting in accord with God's will.

12.3.41 ☐ I can trust in God even when things look dark.
12.3.42 ☐ I can determine where God wants a group to go and help it get there.
12.3.43 ☐ I have a strong desire to take the gospel to places where it has never been heard.
12.3.44 ☐ I enjoy reaching out to new people in my church and community.
12.3.45 ☐ I am sensitive to the needs of people.
12.2.46 ☐ I have been able to make effective and efficient plans for accomplishing the goals of a group.
12.3.47 ☐ I often am consulted when fellow Christians are struggling to make difficult decisions.
12.3.48 ☐ I think about how I can comfort and encourage others in my congregation.
12.3.49 ☐ I am able to give spiritual direction to others.
12.3.50 ☐ I am able to present the gospel to lost persons in such a way that they accept the Lord and His salvation.
12.3.51 ☐ I possess an unusual capacity to understand the feelings of those in distress.
12.3.52 ☐ I have a strong sense of stewardship based on the recognition that God owns all things.
12.3.53 ☐ I have delivered to other persons, messages that have come directly from God.
12.3.54 ☐ I can sense when a person is acting under God's leadership.

12.3.55 ☐ I try to be in God's will continually and be available for His use.

12.3.56 ☐ I feel that I should take the gospel to people who have different beliefs from me.

12.3.57 ☐ I have an acute awareness of the physical needs of others.

12.3.58 ☐ I am skilled in setting forth positive and precise steps of action.

12.3.59 ☐ I like to meet visitors at church and make them feel welcome.

12.3.60 ☐ I explain Scripture in such a way that others understand it.

12.3.61 ☐ I can usually see spiritual solutions to problems.

12.3.62 ☐ I welcome opportunities to help people who need comfort, consolation, encouragement, and counseling.

12.3.63 ☐ I feel at ease in sharing Christ with nonbelievers.

12.3.64 ☐ I can influence others to perform to their highest God-given potential.

12.3.65 ☐ I recognize the signs of stress and distress in others.

12.3.66 ☐ I desire to give generously and unpretentiously to worthwhile projects and ministries.

12.3.67 ☐ I can organize facts into meaningful relationships.

12.3.69 ☐ God gives me messages to deliver to His people.

12.3.70 ☐ I am able to sense whether people are being honest when they tell of their religious experiences.

12.3.71 ☐ I enjoy presenting the gospel to persons of other cultures and backgrounds.
12.3.72 ☐ I enjoy doing little things that help people.
12.3.73 ☐ I can give a clear, uncomplicated presentation.
12.3.74 ☐ I have been able to apply biblical truth to the specific needs of my church.
12.3.75 ☐ God has used me to encourage others to live Christ like lives.

MASTER TEACHING EDITION

ALL AVAILABLE AT OUR GIFT SHOP ON THE WEB

We would love to help you write your dreams down. Each story is precious let White Marlin Media make yours known. Allow us to serve your needs with your family or Christian work: Poetry, stories, textbooks, children's books, we live to serve you. To order other books by this author, send

michaeldonaldson@asharaministries.com

or shop the web at
https://www.asharaministries.com/ashara-bookstore/

BIBLIOGRAPHY
BECOMING A MORE EFFECTIVE TEACHER

      I would like to thank every contributor to this work. I cited more than #60 works, compilations and or sources to make the point that gut feelings are simply not enough to certify and verify Kingdom workers. Benevolence, has it place, but teaching in the kingdom is no longer has a place for it any longer.

[1] For more information log onto www.asharaministries.com.
[2] John 14:9, Matthew 28:16-20.
[3] https://www.google.com/search?ei=roLOWreKFcLgjwSY-JoDQ&q=why+is+is+called+a+masters+degree&oq=why+is+is+called+a+masters+degree&gs_l=psy-ab.3..33i22i29i30k1l9.6071.16780.0.17534.36.34.0.0.0.0.307.4391.0j15j6j2.23.0....0...1c.1.64.psy-ab..21.1.138....0.ZIHpaCY5scc
[4] Matthew 28:20.
[5] Ephesians 4:3
[6] Ephesians 4:11.
[7] Psalms 22:3.
[8] The Lights in Patmos, Michael Donaldson.
[9] Authority https://en.wikipedia.org/wiki/Authority_(sociology)
[10] Strong's Numbers are an index of every word in the original biblical texts. Each Strong's Number links the root meaning of the words of the Bible back to the original meanings in the Hebrew and Greek manuscripts from which they were translated, Strong's Exhaustive Concordance of the Bible. Abingdon Press, 1890.
[11] 1 Peter 4:17.
[12] The references in the book preceded by H (Hebrew) or G (Greek) and containing number are Strong's numbers. Strong, James. Strong's Exhaustive Concordance of the Bible. Abingdon Press, 1890. Print.
[13] https://www.catholic.org/saints/angels/angelchoir.php, 07/11/2018.
[14] Matthew 19:17.
[15] The Lights in Patmos, Michael Donaldson Shepard's Ink Pub, 2008.
[16] Judges 9:8-15.

[17] https://www.blueletterbible.org/lang/Lexicon/Lexicon.cfm?strongs=G348&t=KJV

[18] https://www.forbes.com/sites/deeppatel/2017/03/22/11-powerful-traits-of-successful-leaders/#6b1cb744469f

[19] John 6:37.

[20] Galatians 1:8-9.

[21] Ezekiel 13:9 / Jeremiah 23:16 / Luke 6:26 / Matthew 16:11-3 / 2 Timothy 4:3-4 / Acts 20:28-30 /

2 Peter 3:14-18 / 1 John 4:1-6 / Matthew 7:15-20 / 2 Peter 1:3-21 / Titus 1:6-16 / 2 Peter 2 / Matthew 23:1-29

[22] Ezekiel 13:9 / Matthew 7:15 / Matthew 24:24 / Luke 6:26 / First John 4:1 / Second Peter 2:1-3 / Mar 13:22.

[23] Jeremiah 23:16 / Jeremiah 14:14 / Jeremiah 23:32 / Ezekiel 21:23 / Zechariah 11:2 / 2 Corinthians 11:3 / Galatians 2:4 / 1 Timothy 4 / 2 Timothy 3:3 / 1 John 4 / Revelations 19:20 / Revelations 20:11 / Isaiah 3:2 / Isaiah 9:16 / Isaiah 29:21 / Micah 3:5 / Jeremiah 50:6 / Matthew 24:11 / Colossians 2:4.

[24] https://en.wikipedia.org/wiki/Credential

[25] A very brief history of credentialing, Elizabeth Scoville and James S. Newman, FACP. https://acphospitalist.org/archives/2009/05/newman.htm.

[26] Traits of piety, pride, and conceited; antithetical to compassion and stewardship.

[27] James 5

[28] Colour Tones for Education, http://www.colorobjects.com/en/color-columns/the-color-real/item/357-psychology-of-color-in-the-educational-environment.html.

[29] 13 Key Questions - How to Write a Sermon, http://www.bible-study-lesson-plans.com/how-to-write-a-sermon.html.

[30] 15 Things pastors need to stop right now, https://www.propreacher.com/15-things-pastors-need-stop-now.

[31] www.https://bible.org/article/questionnaire-pastoral-candidate

[32] What are the common characteristics of prophets? www.https://iblp.org/questions/what-are-common-characteristics-prophets, Institute in Basic Life Principles.

[33] 1 Corinthians 3:8

[34] 1 Chronicles 11:9-14, 1 Samuel 28:6-11, Exodus 22:18, Leviticus 19:31, Galatians 5:19-21, Micah 5:3, Deuteronomy 18:11-14, Ecclesiastes 3:5-9, Ecclesiastes 9:4-6

[35] 2 Chronicles 33:6

[36] English Standard Version

[37] Five Movements: Winning the Battle for Your Prophetic Gift by Marko Joensuu, Iheringius (January 15, 2014)

[38] What are the common characteristics of prophets? www.https://iblp.org/questions/what-are-common-characteristics-prophets, Institute in Basic Life Principles.

[39] https://www.biblestudytools.com/dictionary/evangelist, 05/16/2018.

[40] 4 Free Evangelism Tools Everyone Must Have, https://www.evangelismcoach.org/4-free-evangelism-tools-everyone-must.

[41] www.http://oga.pcusa.org/site_media/media/uploads/oga/pdf/examinationsampling.pdf

[42] https://en.wikipedia.org/wiki/Deaco.

[43] 3 things I tell the deacons, Joe McKeever. http://joemckeever.com/wp/3-deacons.

[44] 7 Habits of Highly Effective Deacons, by Mike Mazzalongo https://bibletalk.tv/7-habits-of-highly-effective-deacons

[45] https://www.google.com/search?ei=tygIW9utHsLc9AOqwJaYBA&q=what+is+a+church+elder&oq=what+is+a+church+elder&gs_l=psy-ab.1.0.0j0i7i30k1j0l2j0i30k1j0i8i30k1l5.5322.6348.0.8555.7.7.0.0.0.0.248.831.0j2j2.4.0....0...1c.1.64.psy-ab..4.3.650...0i8i7i30k1.0.jdvmeah66fo

[46] What are the duties of an elder in the church?, by Alexander Strauch. https://www.gotquestions.org/duties-elder-church.html

[47] 7 Habits of Highly Effective Deacons, by Mike Mazzalongo https://bibletalk.tv/7-habits-of-highly-effective-deacons

[48] www.http://www.watermark.org/blog/36-theological-questions-ask-elders-ask

[49] For such a time as this, http://calledforsuchatimeasthis.blogspot.com/2011/04/responsibilities-of-apostle-by-paul.html. 04/18/18.

⁵⁰ Characteristics of the Apostolic Preaching in Acts, https://www.leadershipresources.org/blog/characteristics-apostolic-preaching-book-acts.

⁵¹ 11 Characteristics of Christ's True Apostles, Joseph Mattera. https://www.charismanews.com/opinion/44847-11-characteristics-of-christ-s-true-apostles

⁵² What is Learning Style?, Dr Rita Dunn. http://www.ilsa-learning-styles.com/Learning+Styles/What+is+Learning+Style.html.

⁵² Mosston's styles of teaching: a review of command style, http://www.freepatentsonline.com/article/VAHPERD-Journal/228909097.html

⁵³ What is Learning Style?, Dr Rita Dunn. http://www.ilsa-learning-styles.com/Learning+Styles/What+is+Learning+Style.html

⁵⁵ 5 tips for witnessing to atheists. By Lonnie Wilkey. http://westernrecorder.org/1466.article.

⁵⁶ 5 Big Things We Get Wrong When Talking to Atheists about God, https://www.crosswalk.com/blogs/christian-trends/5-big-things-we-get-wrong-when-talking-to-atheists-about-god.html

⁵⁷ 11 facts about atheists, Michael Lipka. http://www.pewresearch.org/fact-tank/2016/06/01/11-facts-about-atheists/

⁵⁸ Teaching Styles, Center for Teaching Excellence. https://www.sc.edu/about/offices_and_divisions/cte/teaching_resources/goodteaching/teaching_styles/

⁵⁹ 1 Corinthians 9:19-23.

⁵⁹ The Style of a Speech: Speaker, Audience & Purpose, Study.com. https://study.com/academy/lesson/the-style-of-a-speech.html

⁶⁰ 5 Signs You Have Bad Interpersonal Skills, Sheera Hussin. https://leaderonomics.com/personal/5-signs-bad-interpersonal-skills

⁶¹ Mosston's styles of teaching: a review of command style, http://www.freepatentsonline.com/article/VAHPERD-Journal/228909097.html

⁶² The 67 Worst Teaching Mistakes, http://oncourseworkshop.com/table-contents/67-worst-teaching-mistakes/

⁶³ Walker, L. W. (2008). Learning lessons on lessons learned. Paper presented at PMI® Global Congress 2008-North America, Denver, CO. Newtown Square, PA: Project Management Institute.

[64] 11 Keys to Writing A Speech, Jeff Schmitt. https://www.forbes.com/sites/jeffschmitt/2013/07/16/11-keys-to-writing-a-speech/#11b9c69a4fb7

[65] 13 Steps to Effective Lesson Planning for Grades 7-3 https://www.thoughtco.com/write-lesson-plans-8035.

[66] 11 Steps to Better Lesson Plans, Kelly Tenkely. http://teaching.monster.com/benefits/articles/9177-11-steps-to-better-lesson-plans.

[67] Why Colors and Shapes Matter, Ellen Booth Church. http://www.scholastic.com/browse/article.jsp?id=3746476

[68] How to Choose the Best Colors for your Presentations, Kelly Morr. https://blog.prezi.com/choose-the-best-colors-for-presentations

[52] The 8 Learning Styles: Which One Works for You? Nayomi Chibana. http://blog.visme.co/8-learning-styles/

[70] Nine Gifts of the Holy Spirit, Benny Hinn. https://www.bennyhinn.org/nine-gifts-of-the-holy-spirit/.

[70] Discover Your Spiritual Gifts! https://www.lifeway.com/lwc/files/lwcf_pdf_discover_your_spiritual_gifts.pdf. 2018.

[71] Discover Your Spiritual Gifts! by Gene Wilkes. https://www.lifeway.com/lwc/files/lwcf_pdf_discover_your_spiritual_gifts.pdf.

[72] Ken Hemphill, Serving God: Discovering and Using Your Spiritual Gifts Workbook (Dallas: The Sampson Company, 1995), Your Spiritual Gifts Can Help Your Church Grow by C. Peter Wagner, Copyright © 1979, Regal Books, Ventura, CA 93003. Used by permission.

[73] Ken Hemphill, Serving God: Discovering and Using Your Spiritual Gifts Workbook (Dallas: The Sampson Company, 1995), Your Spiritual Gifts Can Help Your Church Grow by C. Peter Wagner, Copyright © 1979, Regal Books, Ventura, CA 93003. Used by permission.

www.ingramcontent.com/pod-product-compliance
Lightning Source LLC
Chambersburg PA
CBHW060509300426
44112CB00017B/2602